The
TURNING POINT

The TURNING POINT

Moments that changed lives

EDITED BY GARETH ST JOHN THOMAS

First published 2021

Exisle Publishing Pty Ltd
PO Box 864, Chatswood, NSW 2057, Australia
226 High Street, Dunedin, 9016, New Zealand
www.exislepublishing.com

A CiP record for this book is available from the National Library of Australia.

ISBN 978 1 922539 02 1

Designed by Enni Tuomisalo
Typeset in PT Serif, 10pt
Printed in China

This book uses paper sourced under ISO 14001 guidelines from well-managed forests and other controlled sources.

10 9 8 7 6 5 4 3 2 1

CONTENTS

Introduction

GARETH ST JOHN THOMAS

Can just one moment change your life? Or is any moment, no matter how significant, just a culmination of previous experience? Or was Shakespeare right with his famous quote: 'There is a tide in the affairs of men, which taken at the flood, leads on to fortune. Omitted, all the voyage of their life is bound in shallows and in miseries. On such a full sea are we now afloat. And we must take the current when it serves, or lose our ventures.'

Writers, being normally reflective people, seek to live examined lives. We see in this anthology how writers' turning-point moments fit into their own self-narratives and are reminded that history, no matter how seemingly inevitable, is often made with surprising materials.

The discovery of wonder, love, one's own agency, courage and beauty all appear here in a range of experiences as diverse as humanity. While some moments clearly were adventures and bolts from the blue delivering instant change, others are more obviously the fulcrum of smoother developments. From stray bullets in Los Angeles, love on the Australian plains, dodging Nazis in Europe, telling a doctor 'no' to finding fairies in granny's garden, you will find much to enjoy and think about.

This anthology was born of an international writing competition. Writers sometimes need accessible challenges to get them up and typing, and the competition asked them to write about a turning point in their life. The writing astonished us — it was as if the writers had taken note of the English poet Sir Philip Sydney's muse simply instructing, 'look in thy heart and write'.

Gareth St John Thomas
Ngātīmoti
February 2021

ABOUT THE COMPETITION

In 2020 the Exisle Academy launched a writing competition open to all, with the challenge being to write about a turning point in life. There were hundreds of entries, many of a very high standard. As well as the four winners, we have included thirty-five competition entries in this book. Many that were excluded were also of a high standard but their experiences are, to the initiated reader, of a very similar nature to those that are already included.

Find out more about the Exisle Academy on the website:
exisleacademy.com

Gareth St John Thomas

PART 1
LOVE AND ROMANCE

Ye gods! Annihilate but space and time.
And make two lovers happy.

Alexander Pope

4

To be wise and love
Exceeds man's might.

William Shakespeare

*N*early all of us experience romance at some point of our lives. For some, romance consumes their very being; for others, it is a ship that passes by that they jump on for just a while. While some affairs of the heart seem complicated and surprising to those looking from the outside, others seem to fit with the natural order of things. Marjorie Counsel's golden hued, and prize-winning, story of when she was proposed to is a good example of this; there is a sense of place and time, and a touch of wistfulness as her memory is captured. Vicky Lopez, a competition-winning author, felt the 'leaden weight of embodied memory' being lifted at her first embrace with an unexpected lover — her sense of surprise at the critical moment is shared by other writers in this section. Stephanie Percival never thought that the note on her windscreen would bring positive life changes. Did Roy Innes really not expect to be 'smitten and overwhelmed by this little life that would change his — forever'? Meryl Broughton brings to life the pace and change, and perhaps the final predictability, of the dating world, while Gwyneth Jones' story of unexpected love and companionship in her seventies elegantly reminds us that life has marvellous twists and turns. Most fortunate of all, perhaps, is Cedric Watts, who at the last moment lucked his way into a party and fluked a brief private conversation with a then attached girl who later became his wife.

A farmer's wife?

MARJORIE COUNSEL

I'm ninety years old, and five years a widow, but the moment that would change my life forever remains crystal clear.

The year was 1952 and I had secured my first teaching job. It was in a remote country town, a three-hour journey from Fremantle, Western Australia, where I grew up. The north-eastern wheat belt was dry and possessed a harsh beauty that took some getting used to. All in all, it was quite a big adjustment for a city girl. But I was young and prepared for new adventures.

Among those adventures, of course, was the prospect of romance. Like many another young teacher or nurse doing country service, I was a potential catch. There may have been many prospects, but it was a gentle, shy young man who caught my eye and we started going steady.

One night, after we had been together for six months, he mentioned, 'There's a dance on next Saturday. How about it?' This was courtship in the classic laconic Aussie tradition!

'Why, that would be nice,' I replied, accepting his invitation as if it was the only answer to give. 'Where will it be? Here?'

'No, down the road — you know, where the hotel is.'

'Oh yes, I know. What time?'

'Better make it 7.30. It's harvest time, you know. I won't come in from the paddock until late.'

'That's fine by me,' I agreed, as we walked to the car beneath a big orange ball, suspended above the horizon — the harvest moon; so romantic, so unreal. Sitting next to this man who was a stranger to me not so many months before. I still hardly knew him and yet at the same time it was as if I had known him forever. 'How can you go to a dance after working on the tractor all day?' I wanted to know.

He answered with a chuckle, 'Don't worry, I'll be right … '

And right on time he called for me at the home in town where I was boarding. I thought he looked very handsome.

Country dances are a whole lot of fun and a great outing for a courting couple. The evening flew by and was over too soon.

'We're here already,' he said, as he pulled up at my gate. We walked slowly arm in arm up the path. I felt sad that the weekend was ending much too quickly. Although I really didn't want him to leave, I had to be firm. 'I must go,' I said reluctantly. I was thinking of the morning with the class preparation that was to be done, so with a light kiss and heavy determination I said goodnight.

Not too many months later, the 'big moment' came. This day, as we had done so often before, we went out driving in his father's gleaming new Austin. When we pulled up in the far paddock of his parents' farm we sat close to each other. It was then the young lover turned and asked for my hand in marriage in true Aussie style.

'Let's get hitched?'

I looked out at what was a typical wheat belt scene — small sand dunes scattered along the perimeter, bordered by the leafy Mallees, where rabbits bounded through the scrub. All of this strange new world would be my home if I said 'yes'.

'Look!' he suddenly whispered, drawing my attention to a stately kangaroo as it jumped out from behind the Mallees, drew itself up to its full height and cautiously scanned the horizon before slowly hopping towards us. Hardly breathing, we watched.

'I haven't seen anything like this,' he continued in astonishment as the roo moved slowly forward.

'Will it reach the car?' I asked, also in a whisper.

'Shh …' he cautioned, but it was too late. Suddenly aware that we were there, our surprise visitor turned, disappearing in a cloud of dust.

'Oh no!' I slumped back, allowing the silence to surround and separate us.

Slowly my companion turned towards me again and taking hold of both my hands in his, said, 'Don't let this spoil our special moment.'

'You're right,' I ruefully replied, pausing to add, 'I'll remember this day, though; the day my boyfriend let a kangaroo take preference over me and my marriage proposal.'

'Well, are you going to?' he persisted.

'Going to what?' I countered, pretending ignorance.

'Get married, of course.' By this time, he'd started the car and his attention was now on the road, steering through loose sand until he pulled up in the paddock where Molly, Rose and Daisy grazed contentedly.

I smiled, putting my arm around him. 'On one condition.'

'What's that?' he wanted to know.

'I don't have to milk the cows!'

Skin to sea

VICKY LOPEZ

I had never swum in the ocean before. Having spent the past four years living along the coast in Santa Barbara, I often evaded the task by sitting silently on the sand, admiring the crashing waves from a distance, ignoring the pleas from my friends to join them in the cool water. I was afraid of drowning.

It was the 4th of July. Back then, I had made a custom of drinking so much that most nights were indiscernible and my memories were replaced by pieced-together recollections of stories my friends would share with me. There are many moments I don't remember, but I remember this day — my first step in ocean water, the first touch of skin to sea. This was the moment that changed my life.

I spent a lot of my young life afraid. As my mother's relationship with my father unravelled, she sought solace in the rigidity of the teachings of the Baptist Church. This left me, her devout and faithful daughter, confined to her religious expectations. I spent almost every day of every week in Church.

In addition to my learning of the books and stories of the Bible, the Church taught me to fear everything that I believed unexplainable. Flickering lights suggested the presence of a demon, sudden changes in temperature meant there were ghosts nearby, and waking up in the middle of the night unprompted signified an ungodly presence in the room. Maybe they were superstitions driven by a child's imagination, or the consequence of lecturing to ten-year-olds about the Apocalypse, but I could not escape that crushing feeling of absolute, unending terror.

As I grew older and unearthed aspects of my identity, and simultaneously uncovered the hypocrisy of religious love, I made the decision to leave the Church and detach myself from the lessons I had grown up with. I couldn't, however, detach myself from the unshakeable fear that the Church had embedded so deeply within my being. Following teenage trysts and sapphic desires, this fear evolved into a nauseating, stomach-turning sense of self-contempt. Former Sunday School teacher and Bible School leader, I knew better than anyone else that my god couldn't love a child like me. And what is left to console the impious and irreligious when not even the all-loving can love you?

As a symptom of this newly acquired self-disgust, I was never very careful with myself. I left for college too naive, too afraid of myself, too willing to take risks without my own wellbeing in mind. I have always blamed myself. I think until recently I've been unable to point that blame elsewhere, only inwards, where I could scream and scramble with my affliction privately.

When I was eighteen, I was raped by an acquaintance at a frat party. It was very simple. I had been drinking. I remember being told to be quiet, the sting of my shoulders hitting the porcelain edge of the toilet and the bluish bruises that resulted. I remember some stranger's panicked voice as he ordered me an Uber home, attempting to decipher my slurred speech as I recited my address. I remember crying as I arrived to see my roommates, my shirt untied and undergarments soaked in blood and vomit, too ashamed to explain the cause of my distress. I remember awaking the next morning, wishing I hadn't told anyone at all, as though it would make it all feel less real.

The weight of the event left me disgusted with my own body. I didn't see how I could be worth a police report, worth an investigation, worth even any kind of sympathy. I avoided grief through self-displacement — frequenting the beds of men whose names I did not know, seduced by the belief that they could not hurt me if I was the one to let them have me. I relied on liquor to feign the appearance of fortitude and stumbled through the week remembering only a handful of the events of each evening.

I was lost. Sex for me was no longer about pleasure, or love, or connection. More than anything, it was about control. It was a desperate attempt to find desire, to reclaim the body that I was too afraid to love as my own. I gave away bits and bits of myself until I started to doubt there was anything else left anymore.

I had known her for some time prior to the 4th of July; we had spent significant time together as friends-of-friends or peers or study partners, but nothing more. At the risk of sounding clichéd and unimaginative, I tell you now that I always knew I would fall in love with her. But I was afraid then — of being in love, of learning desire, of not being enough to allow her to feel the same. I was afraid of drowning.

On the 4th, emboldened by the spirit of the holiday (and perhaps the drinking that had taken place that afternoon), I invited her to a walk to the beach. As we neared the water, with the sun gently kissing our skin and warming our hearts, I revealed to her how much I longed to be enveloped in her love. Her presence alleviated the crushing feeling that life was an endless burden and let me for a moment believe that, somewhere inside me, I knew what love was.

I remember our first embrace, the first touch of her lips to mine, the thrill of being alone with the person you most desire. I remember the comfort of her small hands cradled in my own, the radiance of her skin under the setting sun, the pungent smell of coastal air as we neared the sea.

That was the first time I stepped into the ocean. With her, the leaden weight of embodied memory was momentarily lifted, my fear and self-disgust no longer serving to suffocate me. It did not matter that I could not swim. The ocean's waters lapped and grazed at my hip bones and I revelled in the understanding of what it meant to be free.

Note from the blue

STEPHANIE PERCIVAL

The moment that changed my life was not accompanied by thunderclaps, fireworks or cymbals as one might expect from a life-changing moment. In fact, it was a very ordinary day. What could be life-changing about a piece of paper slipped under a windscreen wiper?

There I was, a young woman, still a bit sleepy, halfway on her commute to work. It was a late summer Monday morning, the sky cloudy. I may have been late. I recall I was feeling pretty grumpy. The route was pleasant enough, following lanes winding through the Northamptonshire countryside. The hedges were green, and beyond them harvested fields of stubble. Then, as is normal for late summer in England, it started to spit with rain. I grumbled some more and put on the windscreen wipers. As I did so, I noticed a scrap of paper caught in one.

My mood darkened further as I suspected it was a message from a neighbour complaining I had parked in the wrong place.

I had only moved to Northampton a few weeks before. My reason for the move was a job promotion. I'd left the hubbub of London, commuting on public transport and living in a shared house, to driving my own car and living alone for the first time in my life. I'd set up home in a third-floor rented flat in a cul-de-sac with several other modern blocks and with a communal parking area below.

The piece of paper fluttered. I could have just let it blow away but I thought it might be important. I pulled the car over and grabbed the folded sheet. I'd take a look at it later.

I forgot about the note during the morning and it was midday before I got round to reading the message. And it wasn't what I expected. On a page that looked as it was torn out from an exercise book, written in ink was something along the lines of 'I've seen you in the carpark, come and have a coffee with me sometime'. So it was from a neighbour, and not a complaint but an invitation. His address was a flat in the adjoining block to mine.

My first thought was that this was from some sort of weirdo guy watching me from his flat. But then again, it could be from somebody just wanting to be friendly to a new neighbour.

I've not always found it easy to make friends; I'd told myself that, when I moved from London to my new job, if I was invited out for a meal or coffee I would do it. I'd thought that kind of offer would come from my new colleagues, not this out-of-the-blue type of invite. Now I had a decision to make. Would I keep that promise to myself to be sociable … or not?

I did what any sensible twenty-something-year-old woman would do. In my lunch hour I went out and bought a book on graphology.

In these days of emails and texts, graphology — the study and analysis of handwriting — is a dying art. But PCs and smartphones were a while away in the mid-1980s. Over the next couple of days, I studied the handwriting. Conveniently, there was a section on 'The action of the compulsive, deluded or mentally disturbed'. I could find none of the telltale traits in the handwriting displayed. There were no backward facing loops or 'repression in the under-strokes' that would indicate a psychopath. After some deliberation I concluded that it was written by an educated man who liked literature.

I decided I'd take my chances.

My first impressions were not great — there had been a fire in the stairwell of my neighbour's block so the staircase and door of the flat were blackened and a smoky smell remained.

I knocked on the door and waited. After a few moments the door opened. The bloke standing there looked remarkably 'normal'. He invited me in. His walls were lined with books on makeshift brick-and-plank shelving. It turned out that he was an English teacher who had studied postgrad literature. I silently applauded myself on my accurate reading of his handwriting sample.

We had that first coffee.

My neighbour told me later that it was an unusual thing for him to have done, writing a note and putting it on a stranger's car.

I won't elaborate on the relationship that gradually developed from friendship to romance. But suffice to say we have just celebrated our 33rd wedding anniversary.

As I said at the start, the moment that changed my life was not accompanied by thunderclaps, fireworks or cymbals. However, it intrigues me that the life-changing moment came about when two people acted out of character, and the fact that a scrappy piece of paper did not blow away when the windscreen wipers started to move.

Perhaps I just didn't hear the thunder.

A new life

ROY INNES

I'm a throwback. I admit it. Back to the days when men were men as the saying goes, male through and through — in thought, word and deed. I have, however, learnt to temper the word and deed parts, a necessity if I want to safely navigate the minefield of modern sentiment.

The trend to unisex is everywhere these days but there are times when a distinct gender difference exists. No better example of this is having a newborn infant thrust upon the scene. Males do not handle this well — at any age.

I distinctly remember my first encounter, forced upon me by my mother when she brought baby sister home from the hospital. I was six years old.

'You can hold her.'

She said this with such an air of loving pride that even at that young age I knew I'd better show some enthusiasm. My father, of course, was a lost cause in this regard. Babies were women's work.

It was awful. Hardly any hair, red face, puffy eyes, a mouth that kept making guppy movements … and a very bad smell. I handed her back as quickly as I could.

Fast forward to the first year of my married life. The subject of children crept insidiously into our conversations, usually after a glass or two of wine. I grew up with two brothers and, along with my sister, we competed for our parents' attention. Frequently, this got ugly and so *family* did not have the same warm, fuzzy feeling for me that it obviously did for my wife — she, an only child.

The screw got turned, ever so slowly. It began with an appeal to my maleness — a strapping son who would play golf and go hunting with me. Sounded good, although I'm in a regular foursome and I've hunted with the same bunch of guys for years. 'You could teach him,' she said. Good move. I like teaching and there certainly were no opportunities to do so in either my golf or hunting groups — hard-nosed egotists, the lot of them.

Her friends were having babies, which, for reasons only a woman would understand, necessitated frequent viewings. 'Ooh, she/he is soooo cute.'

Not so from my point of view. Still red faced and so forth, just like when I was six, and if anything, they smelled worse. Holding them, however, appeared to thrill the women. The rapturous look in my wife's eyes when she did so worried me. Fortunately, no one, even her, expected me to hold the precious things, especially after I let go one of those male bad deed things: an overt grimace of distaste. I was, however, careful not to risk making any descriptive comments. I didn't have to: the women gushed out more than enough of those on their own.

My interest focused on the fathers. Males can read males, I kid you not. To a man, they were embarrassed. I could feel it. Not one 'ooh' from any of them. The closest to any reaction that I could see was the occasional chest puffed out (a successful stud I am, I am).

And the women — merciless. 'When are you two going to start? It will change your lives.'

Change my life? I was quite happy with my life as it was and I didn't appreciate being pushed. Bad deed signs again, which embarrassed my wife. I would pay for those later, but it was worth it.

I stalled as long as I could, but eventually she wore me down. 'We' got pregnant. This instantly gained me acceptance in the when-are-you-going-to-start group. The husbands, however, seemed reserved at the news — unnervingly so.

It didn't take long for me to discover why they reacted that way. Pregnancy is nine months of escalating hell — for both of us. Six weeks of cheery, cheery, happy, happy and then — morning sickness. Three weeks of barfing. Ever tried to sleep in when your dearest is heaving into the toilet, loudly, with the door open?

It got worse. Near the end she was exhausted. No wonder. Trying to move with a basketball in her belly and lug around a 30-pound gain in weight? Would have exhausted me, too. But it was the change in attitude that got me down — a mix of 'I want it all over' and 'damn it, you did this to me'. Not fair.

The last hours were the worst — waves of panic and tons of pain. Fortunately, my presence at the actual birth was a no-go. I told her that, without one iota of doubt, I would pass out and be an unnecessary burden to the medical staff, to say nothing of the indignity of my having to be carried out.

I gave her hand a squeeze when they put her on the stretcher and wheeled her to wherever the last of the suffering takes place. Best I could do.

And then I retired to the waiting room where I sat alone with my thoughts, the major one being, why the hell does any sane pair of human beings voluntarily put themselves through all this? Pregnancy should be an accidental thing, a 'no choice' event — like fire or a flood or any other natural disaster that must be faced should it actually occur.

Her parents joined me near the end of my wait; she bubbling over with joy, he, a man of few words likely wishing he was home watching a hockey game.

Our obstetrician finally appeared, still wearing his greens, mask pulled down. Big smile.

'Your wife's just fine and you are the father of a healthy baby boy. Congratulations. Nurse will bring him around to the viewing window in just a few minutes.'

And there he was — red face, puffy eyes … indistinguishable from his nursery mates nearby. But was he? I thought I could see a bit of his mother in those eyes and that frown surely came from my side of the family. He looked smarter, too, than all the rest, his fleeting gaze taking in the world around him. And just once, I swear he focused on me, wiggling my fingers at him through the glass, his father, smitten and overwhelmed by this little life that would change his — forever.

And to my utter astonishment, I wanted to hold him.

Tall, dark and handsome

~

MERYL BROUGHTON

It was once a stately home close to the city centre. We simply called it 'Francis Street'. I remember wandering over the faded tiles at the front that hinted of a grand patio. The area extended beyond those French doors, opening from a domestic ballroom. I don't suppose it really was a ballroom. I was just small and imaginative while the room and building were relatively large. The house was already dilapidated at the time we had access to it as a place for youth activities.

The most intriguing aspect of the mansion was a cellar. Ordinary houses did not possess secret rooms like this. And in the psychedelic

1960s, it became a favourite hangout for us teenagers, with a décor to match, though we could not add incense to the mood lighting due to fire hazard.

All the girls in the group were waiting weeks for the pastor's oldest son to arrive from over east. The rest of his family had already moved here. He was delayed by his tertiary training schedule and course transfer issues. This heightened our anticipation. What would he be like? I hoped Wendy, the popular girl, wouldn't catch him; she already had the pick of the guys. Eventually the occasion came for his introduction into our society. My prayers were answered: he was tall, dark and handsome, and he didn't like Wendy. He became my first crush.

I pined for and pursued him for six months. The crash finally came and the date indelibly etched in my brain down in that groovy basement at Francis Street. When my best friend caught me staring doe-eyed at my 'intended' that night, she briskly ushered me into the private cubicle under the stairs and heartlessly pierced me, declaring 'He's not at all interested in you, never will be. Stop being stupid. Get over it.'

My infatuation bubble burst. I was simultaneously bereaved and liberated.

Moments later in an act of reckless defiance, I bestowed my first kiss on that guy's younger brother. It was his birthday, after all, and a gift he appreciated.

The mystical power of one point in time is only unveiled looking back. From then on, free from the drive to behave in a particular way and a mould that retrospectively did not fit, my personality took on a more natural shape, though tinged with a Mona Lisa mood.

The very next evening was a social outing in a different setting with a different mix of young people. Another boy met me. I'm sure I wasn't doing any meeting, I wasn't paying particular attention in my altered mental state. But it was clear I'd made a favourable impression because I became the one pursued. Funny how things you want may come to you only when you are not trying so hard to obtain them. This was how I acquired my first boyfriend, with no effort on my part.

In time, a second followed. This next one lived in another town. Having an absent boyfriend gave my interactions with the local boys an interesting degree of freedom. I did not have to impress them — they were already impressed by my having a boyfriend — and they were not afraid of their friendly behaviour towards me being misinterpreted as romantic.

Eventually I broke up with the second guy. Apparently, my destiny was not aligned to his. Rather than relieved, I felt unexpectedly sad about the end of that relationship and change of status, perhaps because I was enjoying the carefree connection to the local boys. Would this be different when they knew I was 'available'?

The youth group was walking from Francis Street to a city cinema for the Friday night activity. As we marched along the route, the leaders checked on their charges, 'Who's at the back of the group?' 'It's just Ian and Meryl, they'll be all right,' meaning we were trusted to behave appropriately.

Four years had passed since that first kiss in the cellar. Ian had grown to be a handsome young man in his own right, similar to but sufficiently different from his older brother. He had been patiently awaiting his opportunity. This outing was the moment he made his move. 'Well, we weren't expecting that,' the leaders later reflected.

It is not an unusual story, that a friendly relationship develops into one of romance. Who can explain the magical process that causes your heart to beat faster when your special someone stands next to you, or the tingling delight when you hear their voice? What creates those rose-coloured glasses with which you view your beloved?

We ultimately got married, got jobs, moved interstate, bought properties and proceeded with life. As happens with these activities, papers need to be signed and Ian was the main paper-handler in our partnership. One typical busy workday, I was expecting him to drop by my place of employment with such an autograph-requiring document.

A phone call came through to my department. 'There's a man waiting for you at the front reception area.'

'Is he tall, dark and handsome?' I cheerily enquired, anticipating the mysterious stranger to be my husband.

'No.'

Suddenly I was surprised. Who could it be then?

I made my wondering way to the foyer. The young receptionist who had rung for my attendance did not see my dear husband the way I obviously still did.

A pink frilly top

⤳

GWYNETH JONES

I was in my seventies and already tucked away in a retirement village
to see out the years I had left in comfort when my moment came.
Off to bed early snuggled up in warm flannelette nightwear was the
highlight of my life that winter. There was morning tea on Tuesday
and bingo in the afternoon, but little else was of much interest to me.
I did the daily crossword in the paper and always had a jigsaw on the
go, and apart from that the days slipped into weeks and life rolled on.

The mid-winter Christmas dinner to be held at the RSA was advertised
in the June village social calendar so I entered my name as to be

attending — might as well give it a whirl as I didn't go to much else. What to wear became the problem now that I had committed myself to this outing and my wardrobe looked pretty dismal, so I decided I might as well cancel going to the dinner. I wasn't prepared to spend good money on a new outfit to be worn for a two-hour dinner at the RSA. As I went to close the wardrobe door I noticed, lying in a heap on the floor, a pink frilly top with tiny white spots that my granddaughter had forgotten to take after her last visit with me. 'I'll try it on for a lark,' I giggled and slipped the gorgeous little garment over my head.

Hey, that doesn't look too bad, I thought, as I whirled back and forth taking in the image in the mirror. It had been many years since I had worn such a delicate piece of clothing and the pink frilly top looked great with my round-the-house jeans, which were fairly new anyway. I wondered if I dared wear it to the dinner. I slipped on my navy jacket with Air Force memorabilia pinned to the lapel and again I was impressed. The colours went well and the pink seemed to reflect colour into my face. But would I have the brass neck to wear such a modern outfit to the mid-winter dinner for the elderly? All month I agonized over what the other female residents would think, but deep down I liked the combination and really wanted to wear it. I was in two minds as my thoughts slid to and fro, from 'What does it matter what others think?' to 'I'll look like mutton dressed up as lamb'.

The day of the dinner finally came around and on trembling, jean-covered legs with frilly pink top, with feet encased in the only pair of high heels that had escaped being sent to the op shop, I made my way through the doors of the RSA dining room, keeping my eyes straight ahead, very aware of glances from those already seated.

The food trays were wheeled in and the manager called for ladies born in the 1930s to line up first. As I stood waiting to fill my plate, a man, who I did not recognize, called to me. 'You've jumped the queue lady. They called for 1930s.'

With all eyes seemingly trained on me, I replied indignantly, 'I was born in 1936!' and moved on with my trembling legs barely holding me up. After slopping a bit of meat and veg onto my plate I returned to my seat but couldn't eat anything. I felt such a fool. It had been a huge mistake to wear such an outfit to a senior do. I would probably be the joke of the village for months now. I couldn't stay any longer, so I picked up my handbag and fled out the door, then leaning against the building wall the tears began to flow.

An arm slid around my shoulder and a voice said, 'I'm so sorry. I didn't mean to upset you.' It was the man who had made the comment about me being in the wrong queue.

'I wasn't criticizing you,' he said apologetically. 'I was complimenting you because you looked so lovely. I thought you were one of the village staff who had come to help and you don't look anywhere near 70 years old.'

He offered me an ironed white hankie, then escorted me into the RSA bar. After buying me a gin and tonic to settle my distress he explained that his name was Barry and he was a new resident having just moved into the village the last week.

'I noticed you as soon as you walked through the door,' he said. 'It was like seeing an exotic flower bloom in a desert of grey sand and I thought, "That lady can't live in the village. She's too young."'

I couldn't help laughing at his description 'exotic flower', which seemed a bit over the top. He continued telling me how taken he was with my outfit and that he would very much like to see me again.

That was the moment that changed my life.

The flannelette nighties were quickly replaced with shimmering satin and lace lingerie. Out went the dowdy contents from my wardrobe and in came trendy jeans, classy shoes and frilly tops. No more crosswords or jigsaws to fill my days, for there was now no time to spare as we took in the shops and movies and ate at restaurants I'd never heard of, and embarked on several overseas trips.

We had enjoyed five wonderful years of travel and companionship when Barry passed away in April. Not only did he change my whole style of living but he also left me with a legacy of beautiful memories. And all because I was bold enough to wear my granddaughter's trendy top to a stodgy old dinner for the elderly.

A spare seat in the back of the car

CEDRIC WATTS

This happened in March 1963.

I was a research student at Cambridge University, writing a thesis entitled 'Joseph Conrad and R.B. Cunninghame Graham: Their friendship in its literary aspects'. I was dependent on a state grant of £300 per year. (Not bad: a workman's average wage was £10 a week.) For the Easter vacation I had returned to my hometown, Cheltenham, in Gloucestershire, staying at my parents' house. My kind and patient mother and father welcomed me, accommodated me and fed me. There was nothing to keep me in Cambridge that vacation, for I had broken my relationship with a girlfriend. More precisely, she had spurned me in order to pursue a relationship with a man who was bigger, taller and prosperous, a thriving young businessman. So I felt lonely and depressed.

I was 26. I had stayed at school till I was eighteen, at last winning a scholarship to Cambridge. Between 1956 and 1958 I did my National Service. I served in the Royal Navy, and my time there included the brief, nightmarish spell of action called the Suez War. Then I took my degree at Cambridge and proceeded to research.

The first Saturday evening of that vacation, I went to my favourite pub, the Restoration, in the hope of meeting old school friends. It was a popular, crowded pub on the High Street. The public bar was full of smoke from cigarettes and pipes. That smoke formed broad bluish-grey planes like stacks of horizontal cloud that you could part with your hand, so that it swirled before stabilizing. I drank a couple of pints of bitter. It was Bass, which always had a faint aroma of bad eggs. And I smoked Senior Service, a strong cigarette, rationing myself to one cigarette with each pint.

I talked to four of my former school friends. Dave Antony, a good-natured fellow; Jack Pierce, a sportsman; and Ian and Paul Green, both rather cynical in outlook. Their conversation was guarded. I noticed that all four had shopping bags containing bottles. I guessed that they were on their way to a party, but they didn't invite me along. Whereas I'd gone to university, they had jobs with local firms, so there was now some distance between us. But I had retained my Gloucestershire accent, so I could blend in with their rhotic conversation, saying 'ar' for 'yes', for instance. And we chuckled over the news from parliament: Defence Minister John Profumo had denied any 'impropriety' in his relationship with Christine Keeler. Of course, he was lying, as we all guessed, and eventually he would have to resign in disgrace. He was in the government of Harold Macmillan, the Prime Minister who told the people, 'You never had it so good.'

Near closing time, the four friends glanced at each other, stood up, raising the bags in which heavy bottles clinked and clunked, and went out, waving farewells to me. I sat by myself, feeling morose, abandoned and unwanted. Then, through the window, I could see that outside in the High Street they were having an argument as they stood beside Dave Antony's car, an old Austin 12. I saw the argument conclude: Jack nodded, and Ian and Paul shrugged, as if to say, 'Fair enough. Do it if you want to.' Then Dave Antony walked back to the pub. He just put his head round the doorway and said to me: 'All right. Come along. I've got a spare seat in the back of the car.' That moment transmuted depression into hope.

Rejuvenated, I hurried out and squeezed into the back of the Austin 12 with its slippery, brown leather upholstery. I sat squashed between Ian and Paul, and we drove north to Montpellier Terrace. We climbed the stairs. The party was on the top floor, in a big flat. Turbulent crowds of young people, smoky atmosphere and glasses tinkling. My need for a girlfriend became an insistent pressure, a yearning hunger. I looked around to see if there were any spare females. I could see just one lone woman: a slim blonde, who was standing over the record player, preoccupied, choosing a record. In the noisy crowd she seemed quietly detached, in her own island of thoughtful silence, almost as though posing in profile for an artist. I gazed, fascinated by that strange self-contained pose.

Then she started the record, and at once the room was full of loud, familiar, boisterous music: a two-year-old hit, *Let's Twist Again*, sung by Chubby Checker. All around, couples were now dancing energetically, for of course they were doing the twist, a simple gyratory exercise which even I could do. I hurriedly walked over and said to the lone young woman, 'Hello. Would you care to dance?' She nodded, and we danced for a while. During that time, I introduced myself and learnt that she, Judith, was a trainee nurse sharing with two other nurses a flat near Pittville Park. 'Might I — take you out for tea — tomorrow afternoon?' I enquired, panting as I twisted. ('Tea' sounds innocuous, an unthreatening invitation that's hard to refuse.) She agreed, and I arranged to meet her the next day.

At this point, her boyfriend, who had been using the lavatory, re-entered the room, elbowed me aside and resumed dancing with her.

The peremptory call of his bladder had permitted my introduction to Judith.

The next day, I was somewhat late in reaching her flat to take her out. I forget why. She was eager, radiant and relieved, for she had thought I had forgotten. But as I pointed out, it was six o'clock so the pubs were opening, so we went for drinks at the upstairs bar at the Plough in the High Street, a quiet, civilized bar with bowls of peanuts on the tables. She said with a sigh, 'I might have guessed that the invitation to tea was too good to be true,' but she forgave me. She had an engaging smile that won trust.

We were married for 43 years, until, at the age of 69, after six months of epileptic fits, she died of a brain tumour. Her son was abroad, but her daughter was present, beside me. When choosing music for the funeral, I reluctantly decided against *Let's Twist Again*; instead, I chose the slow movement of Mozart's Clarinet Concerto.

That happened in October 2007.

PART 2
BIG CHANGES

Luck is what happens when
preparation meets opportunity.

Seneca

᛭

There is a tide in the affairs of men.
Which, taken at the flood, leads on to fortune;
Omitted, all the voyage of their life
Is bound in shallows and in miseries.
On such a full sea are we now afloat,
And we must take the current when it serves,
Or lose our ventures.

William Shakespeare

᛭

Never doubt that a small group of thoughtful,
committed, citizens can change the world.
Indeed, it is the only thing that ever has.

Margaret Mead

*B*ig changes come in all shapes and sizes. A stolen car and a bullet fired through a wild Los Angeles night propelled Mark Scheel, in his prize-winning story, into the steaming jungles of Vietnam. Escaping imprisonment or worse, Roger Sharp 's prize-winning story sets the scene in which gun-wielding soldiers in a war-torn African airport lead him to think 'you only pass this way but once but you don't know how long you are staying'. As a nineteen-year-old marine recruit, Bill Younglove found that his oath of office was the moment that changed his life, while Mark Lovell's thrilling story of escape in Europe helped him discover that 'kindness exists in unexpected places'. Surrounded by sharks, Karen Lethlean understood her own 'insignificance when faced with a life-and-death situation'. Kate Marshall Flaherty met a bear, which gave her inspiration through the fog of COVID.

A bullet in the night

MARK SCHEEL

The summer of 1967, having just graduated from college and medically exempt from the military draft, I struck out, as they say, for California and soon found myself in the downtown LA area working in a huge commercial laundry. The hotel where I rented a sleeping room occupied the two floors above a machine shop and was owned and managed by an elderly Japanese widow, 'Mama'. A gentle, unassuming lady of diminutive stature, she had a special assistant who helped her with the building maintenance more or less on a voluntary basis — a tall, middle-aged single man whose room was next to mine. His name was

Hank, but he went by the moniker 'Bulldog' and, considering his square-jawed face, buzz cut and beefy build, that appellation seemed apropos.

Each night on the corner immediately opposite my hall window, a neon sign blinked its inducement above the door of a Hispanic bar and to the right, half a block away, stood a Native American dance hall. One Friday I accepted an offer for overtime at the laundry the next day repainting the flatwork floor, and so I'd forgo catching a bus to Hollywood, which I often did on weekends to take in the artsy action. That Saturday evening, hearing band music blasting out from across the street, I decided to explore both the bar and the dance hall. I had no inkling at that point that at the day's end a life-altering event would unfold.

The clientele of the Hispanic bar consisted mostly of a sparse older crowd, nursing their beers to mariachi tunes blaring out of a jukebox. In contrast, however, the dance-hall patrons were nearly all young Native Americans, drinking and dancing to an amateur rock'n'roll band whose repertoire extended to only three numbers, repeated over and over and over again. Finding nothing there to indulge my fancy, I finished my beer and wiggled my way through the crowd and out the door, heading back to the hotel.

I hadn't been asleep long when I awoke abruptly to the slamming of Bulldog's door and the background din of shouting and yelling rising from the street. I slipped into my jeans and padded out into the hallway to see what had initiated the commotion. Bulldog had pushed up the window and was leaning out looking over the fire escape at the street below. The dance hall had let out, and a huge crowd of intoxicated youth swarmed about the parking lot and sidewalks and out into the street. Here and there, fistfights were beginning to erupt. Glass was breaking. Some girls were screaming and crying and trying to separate some of the fighters. 'Jeez, guy,' Bulldog commented. 'Looks like we got ourselves a regular street riot.'

I hopped up onto the window ledge and squatted there where I could survey the scene more clearly. Two security guards were hopelessly attempting to direct traffic out of the dance-hall parking lot. Engines raced and tyres squealed. 'Somebody's gonna get run over,' I declared to Bulldog.

About then, immediately below, an older-model black auto appeared, nudging its way along the street through the crowd. Suddenly, someone bounced a beer bottle off its roof. The vehicle stopped and the driver piled out, an Anglo, fists clenched ready to brawl. Three natives waited on the curb, holding bottles — one had what appeared to be a blade — egging him on. The Anglo turned back to the car, opened the rear door, reached in and pulled out a spike axe and began heading for the curb, dragging it behind him. 'Good God! He's got a fireman's axe,' Bulldog exclaimed.

That was the moment I heard the thunder of a gunshot and was simultaneously aware of broken glass tinkling down on the iron of the fire escape. My first thought was that a security guard must have fired in the air to disperse the mob and somebody threw a bottle clear up and hit the fire escape. Then I turned and saw the bullet hole in the window glass beside my head, and heard Bulldog shout, 'Come back in! They're shooting at us!'

Posthaste I scrambled inside and away from the window. Glass lay all over the hall floor where the second pane had shattered inward from the impact. Bulldog looked at me. 'That didn't miss your head by more than an inch,' he declared.

'I know,' was all I could feebly respond.

The next thing we heard was sirens approaching, and the crowd commenced a flight to the four winds. Only those too beat up or too drunk to run remained when the squad cars and paddy wagon arrived. The black automobile was long gone. The police beat on some with nightsticks and threw some in the paddy wagon. In writing up the report of the shooting, they described me as the victim, Bulldog as the witness — and called it a night.

Upon reflection the next day, Bulldog pieced together what had likely precipitated the shooting. Two hippy-type renters, residing in a room on the floor above ours, had also been at their hall window observing the street fracas below. Their car had been stolen days before, and when the black auto had halted in the middle of the street, they recognized it as theirs and began shouting, 'There's the guys who stole our car!' I hadn't heard them, but Bulldog did. Apparently, someone in the car, packing a pistol and hearing the shouting from the hotel, spotted Bulldog's and my silhouettes, thought we were the ones shouting and decided to silence us. And *bang*, that's how cheap life can be in the street.

The close passing of death's kiss began to haunt my thoughts thereafter. What if I'd positioned myself slightly to the left? What if the bullet had grazed the fire escape and deflected slightly to the right? What if the shooter had had a slightly better aim? What if? What if?

Perhaps, I reasoned in my youthful imagination, if there's a bullet with one's name assigned to it, it will find you wherever you go. Escaping a war zone won't matter. One can't cheat fate. And if there's none, well then, it won't matter where you are or where you go. It will be something else further down the line that will take you. And it was partly that logic, I suppose, and my fertile naiveté, that was responsible for me finding myself, many months later, a Red Cross volunteer sweating in the jungles of Vietnam.

You only pass this way but once

ROGER SHARP

On a scheduled Fokker Friendship flight out of Ikeja to Calabar, Nigeria, I was the lone white man. The other passengers, mostly women and children who were more accustomed to travelling in mammy wagons, were carrying basins, bowls of rice, cassava, soups, stalks of plantain and bananas and the like, mostly on their heads or, like the babies, strapped to their backs in colourful cloth.

Shortly after take-off, the pilot announced the plane had been ordered to divert to Enugu for security clearance.

On arrival the plane was boarded by officious, heavy-handed army personnel. They headed straight for me and demanded to see my passport; I told them I had left it in Lagos.

'This be now Biafra, you do now need passport.'

'Nobody do tell me. I did not think I would need it to fly within the country's boundaries,' I protested.

'Where your bag be?'

'It will be in the hold.'

He ordered me off the plane and they started to unload baggage. Fortunately mine was one of the few suitcases on board and was soon found. They went through everything, spreading it across the runway; they started reading a letter I had received from Linda, my girlfriend, who was working as nanny in America.

'You be American?' the officious officer asked.

'Yeah for sure,' I replied, figuring out the Ebos now hated the British, as our government was supporting the federal government's side of the conflict, and if they wished to be a separate country they would want to keep the Americans happy as they were extracting oil in the Niger Delta. The eastern region is rich in natural resources. Harold Wilson, our prime minister of the day, was pouring arms in to the federal government to keep the country as one. I could see a fight was to be had as Russia was showing support to the east — oh how greedy the world's politicians are.

The officer instructed me to repack my suitcase; he then waved me back on board.

As we came to a halt on Calabar's runway, a rag tag army rushed out with automatic rifles and surrounded the plane. I was very roughly pulled out of the passenger line and told to place my hands on my head, then marched to the terminus building to be placed against an outside wall. I was left with one soldier who had his finger on the trigger of his automatic weapon.

'Where be your officer?' I asked the soldier.

'You do shut up, he do come.'

The adrenaline had kicked in, my arms were aching, I was frightened, shaking and losing control of my bodily functions — everything turned to brown water and I could feel it. It seemed an age before an officer turned up in a commandeered charity Land Rover given to farmers.

'You be British?' the officer sharply asked as he pointed his swagger stick at me.

I felt another lie may not do me any harm. 'I come from the British Isles, but I be Irish,' I blurted out nervously. 'For sure you will see some machinery in the cargo hold,' I continued. 'It was my company that sent this over, didn't they charter the aircraft, they have asked me to come along to repair some machinery at the palm oil factory, do you not see these people, that do come with me, it be my company that get your people back here to their homeland, there be plenty palaver in Lagos.'

Panic had set in. I was rambling and babbled on, making things up in my head as I went along. 'I'd do get work in de township at the palm oil factory and I do be happy to do this and travel back to Lagos so I would.'

I might have said much more nonsense; the Indian pilot had seen the situation and was headed my way.

Oh bloody hell, I thought, *he is not going to confirm any of my stories, and what was the story I told them?* I could hardly remember, I had babbled such a load of unexplainable rubbish.

The officer asked the pilot, 'You do wait for this man to go with you?'

Without hesitation the Indian pilot nodded his head. 'We will do.'

The officer signalled to let me put my hands down. He told his driver to take me to the palm oil factory and wait for me. I told them I would be back in half an hour. I collected my lone suitcase and tool bag off the trolley, jumped in the Land Rover and found I couldn't stop the incontrollable shaking. At the factory I stripped, threw away my soiled shorts and underpants, washed myself in a dirty sink, changed clothes, did nothing to the factory's broken machine and quickly left again to return to the airport, hoping the plane would still be on the runway and praying nothing more would happen. I was relieved to see the plane on the runway with its doorway open and the engines running. I jumped out of the Land Rover, flung my tool bag and suitcase straight in the doorway, and no sooner was I in than we took off.

The plane was empty. Once in the air I walked into the cockpit and profusely thanked the captain and co-pilot for waiting for me. I felt they had saved my life. The pilot turned and said, 'We have to land at Enugu for clearance. You better stay in the cockpit; they never look in here, have you long trousers and a plain shirt in your case?'

While the security checks were being carried out I hung on to a clipboard just in case anybody came through the cockpit door — I would pretend I knew what the chart I was staring at was about. After an agonizing half an hour and a few skipped heartbeats as the cabin door opened and closed, we were soon airborne again. As we flew on to Ikeja airport I found great relief, which had an emotional impact on me for tears welled as I shook hands with these men.

In life sometimes, something extreme has a permanent effect on the way you view your life and the way you live it, and this one was to be mine. I never talk about this particular experience; I had been afraid and thought I was going to die. I never thanked God, as I have never prayed in my adult life, so there was no revelation for me, but the experience did give me a laidback attitude to the way I live my life, for I have found if figures of authority in general do give some grief and concern, I think, yes, they can get irate, yes, they can make my life uncomfortable but that is all they can do, besides locking me up. But that little man with the automatic weapon in his hand could have shot me and wouldn't have given a damn; neither would anybody else in the whole wide world except my family and friends.

So, live a moral life, enjoy what you can whenever you can, even if it is praying. You only pass this way but once, but you don't know how long you are staying.

Just following orders

BILL YOUNGLOVE

'Sir, yes sir!' we all shouted, loudly and in unison as we ran full tilt out of Baltimore's then Friendship Airport. I can only imagine what fellow travellers, civilians, thought, as our DI led us to cattle car semis transporting us to Quantico, Virginia. Believe me, friendship and induction into the Marine Corps had nothing to do with each other.

I muttered to my seatmate, 'Can't believe we just lost our freedom …!' And so it was, for this nineteen year old, with a year of college behind him, as he joined young enlistees from all over, to pursue officer training, via the Platoon Leaders Class (PLC).

Whether it was oppressive heat and humidity (regulated, supposedly, by a three-flag 'exercise allowed' system), rising at dawn in the barracks, or daily assemblages on the parade field for inspection(s), every second was controlled by orders. Even if the Corps Commandant initiated orders, they were carried out by Quonset Hut Drill Sergeants, as ordered by our Second Lieutenant.

Just six months earlier, fearing being drafted, I had decided to enlist — to keep some choice in just how I would serve my country. Right-hand raised, I had intoned the Oath of Enlistment:

I, William Younglove, do solemnly swear that I will support and defend the Constitution of the United States against all enemies, foreign and domestic; that I will bear true faith and allegiance to the same; and that I will obey the orders of the President of the United States and the orders of the officers appointed over me, according to the regulations and the Uniform Code of Military Justice. So help me God.

Those words, spoken by me, almost in rote, in my Michigan hometown, took on much greater — real — meaning as time passed.

During UCMJ classes that summer, I learnt that the Uniform Code of Military Justice superseded — replaced, really — my US Constitutional rights, upheld by US Supreme Court decisions. Violations of the UCMJ were handled by Captain's Mast and possible court martials, which might preclude a jury of one's peers. Officers' oaths themselves do not mention the UCMJ.

Physically, it was tough. If the weekly Thursday 20 mile+ hike, in full gear (some 35 pounds), and often 100+ degree heat with 90 per cent humidity, didn't do one in, the mandatory, periodic, two-hour fire watch and/or two-hour guard duty, during varied nights, left one sleep impaired. During instruction, dozing helmets, smacked by ever-watchful DIs, sent candidates sprawling. Squared away hospital-folded racks and footlockers were a given — else contents were strewn about the barracks by inspecting DIs. Same for uniform maintenance and rifle cleanliness. Failure in the latter could mean court martial.

Supervisors' language consisted of yelling, inches from enlistees' faces, often racist and sexist slogans; words laced with threats. By the time I got to Parris Island, South Carolina, night marches into nearby swamps had, fortunately, largely been discontinued due to recruit drownings.

Interestingly — or ironically — my military discharge came just as Vietnam was 'erupting', when President Johnson greatly increased troop numbers to oppose any possible Viet Cong victory.

In the decades following my own, brief, military experience, I studied the Holocaust and other growing genocides. Such studies raised the essential question: why? That is, why have large numbers of military personnel obeyed one or more charismatic leaders in destroying millions of targeted victims?

German civil servants in the 1920s swore an oath to the Weimar Constitution. However, after President Hindenburg's death in 1934, Reich military servants avowed, 'I swear I will be true and obedient to the Führer of the German Reich and people, Adolf Hitler [supreme commander of the Armed Forces], observe the law and conscientiously fulfil the duties of my office, so help me God.'

What, of course, does swearing such an oath mean? Today in the United States, federal employees, representatives, senators, judges, political appointees, even the vice president and president swear an oath. Interestingly, though, said oath is to the Constitution, not to any religious test or individual. The Presidents' Oath of Office is: 'I do solemnly swear that I will faithfully execute the Office of President of the United States, and will to the best of my ability, preserve, protect and defend the Constitution of the United States.' There are many writers, columnists and analysts today who affirm that official representatives in the US, from the president to the lowest-ranking soldier, swear an oath pledging loyalty not to any ruler, administration or party, but to the Constitution itself.

Beginning in late 1945, a series of Nuremberg trials judged the guilt or innocence of Reich military and officials who fulfilled Hitler's orders. '*Befehl ist befehl*' ('an order is an order') was an often-used defence, including by Adolf Eichmann in 1961.

Subsequent to World War II, various US military personnel have run afoul of laws that circumscribe carrying out orders: the 1968 My Lai Massacre led by Army Lieutenant William Calley; waterboarding attempts in Vietnam during the same time period; the 2003 Iraq Abu Ghraib torture abuse, among others.

What was the case, however, when I served in the Marine Corps?

I saw myself as a servant of the people — carrying on democracy in these United States. Orders given, however, could be — and often were — ambiguous. My experiences taught me that loss of my free will and control of my behaviour could lead me to acts that would be reprehensible to my personal ethical and moral values. I did not see that 'just following orders' could ever be a viable defence. Also, there's the matter of representation itself. The Corps made clear from day one: 'You never, ever, contact your elected officials — for anything.' Communicating with the press, tantamount to whistleblowing, could become a court martial offence.

As I continued to study the Holocaust and genocide, researching, writing, interviewing, teaching, developing materials and travelling the world, I became convinced that young people need to carefully examine the very words in any military and national oath of allegiance to which they may commit. National defence, absolutely essential to the safety and security of everyone in the US, is best carried out by those who understand exactly what they pledge.

Since 1980, all male (including transgender who are born male) US citizens, male immigrants, conscientious objectors and disabled men aged eighteen to 25 must register with the US government Selective Service as a possible prelude to military service. It is a felony not to register.

The American Friends Service Committee's National Youth and Militarism Program lists considerations before signing a Military Enlistment Agreement. In sum, the AFSC advises deciding slowly, including having a witness, examining your own moral feelings, reading the fine print of the *written* enlistment agreement, and realizing the suspension of one's civil liberties.

Most of us face numerous momentous events during our lifetimes. As US citizens we are promised much. We may, in turn, promise to serve our country in many different ways. Few decisions will ever control us, however, as do the legal oaths we swear — and just exactly what they mean. For me, enlisting in the military turned out to be the moment that changed my life the most.

Changing trains

MARK R.C. LOVELL

My mother and I once changed trains in Milan. This was not the best place to do so for British citizens trying to return to the United Kingdom from Romania in March 1940. We had no choice. In the first months of World War II, the major powers glared at each other, building alliances and planning what to do, as opposed to actually doing it. Italy was committing itself to Nazi German leadership but was still independent and officially neutral.

For my mother, this was the anxious part of our journey. For myself, aged five, Milano Centrale was just another large railway station. I couldn't have imagined it would be a turning point in my life.

Porters transferred our luggage from the train that brought us from Bucharest to one taking us to Nice in France. We followed them from one platform to another, to make sure we could find the right seats on the right train when the station grew darker in the late evening. My mother also insisted on being shown exactly where our luggage was stowed.

One of the porters spoke urgently to my mother, in French. Her French was good, but she had very little Italian. 'Be very careful,' he advised her. 'Keep to the sides of the concourse, where there are more people. If anybody asks you a question, always answer in French. Never English.'

We followed this advice. Suddenly we heard a rapid stamping of boots passing down a platform while we made our way across the concourse. This stamping became the background to a rousing military song. The lyrics were unintelligible, but my mother immediately understood the cry that men in black shirts were shouting as a chorus: '*Morte agli Inglesi!*' ('Death to the English!').

She said later that she talked to me a lot just then, so as to appear indifferent. The singing and shouting she treated as background noise. She chattered as mothers do: 'Are you warm enough, Mark? Lots of people in this station, aren't there? Are you hungry? Should we get a bite to eat somewhere?' I understood, somehow, that I needn't say anything in reply.

We found ourselves near a restaurant built into the side of the concourse. Outside, close to the entrance, was a large man in his forties with reddish brown hair. He beckoned to us as we were about to pass him. He moved in step with us and tried several languages: '*Scusate mi, signora; bonjour madame*; I wonder if—' My mother began to move away quickly, clutching my hand. But then he said, very clearly, 'Strand Palace Hotel'.

This was so unexpected that she stopped and said, 'Hello?'

'Hello madam,' he replied. 'Please come into my restaurant. You'll be perfectly safe.'

He led us to some booths at the back, installing us where we couldn't be seen from the entrance.

'Thank you very much,' said my mother. 'Did you say, "Strand Palace Hotel"? In London?'

'Yes indeed,' he told her. 'I worked there nearly four years.'

That had been after basic training as a restaurateur. Curiosity and ambition had drawn him to work in other European cities. He liked London and he liked Londoners. He was less complimentary about much English cooking. 'Now I manage this restaurant,' he said, 'but my kitchen cooks Italian!'

'You speak very good English,' said my mother.

I felt left out of this interchange until he shook hands with me, said, 'Hello Marco!' and asked me to call him Raimondo.

My mother explained where we were going and told him our platform number. She expected he knew about trains and the political situation as well as about restaurants. 'Will it be safe on the train?' she asked, 'I mean, for *us*?'

He wanted to reassure us but he was also realistic. 'Nobody stopped and questioned you when your train reached the border at Trieste?'

My mother shook her head. 'I just showed the guard our tickets.'

'Then you will probably be safe here and at the French border. But use French all you can. Does Marco speak a little French?'

In Bucharest I had attended a French school for young children of journalists, diplomats and people in the arts community. I was proud of what I had learnt. '*Mais oui, monsieur!*' I said. '*Bien sûr.*'

'Bravo Marco,' he smiled. 'But are you hungry? May I get something for you from the kitchen?'

My mother was nervous. She had drawn some Italian lire before travelling, but not much. My father had arranged for her to collect French francs in Nice. Raimondo restored calm by saying everything was on the house. She should keep any Italian money for encouraging the staff on the train to be cooperative.

'Escalopes perhaps? And for Marco?'

'Maybe not for you, Mark,' said my mother. I'd recently had a bad toothache. It had disappeared but until I could see a dentist, 'He mustn't chew too much.'

Raimondo smiled. 'I make good omelettes,' he claimed. And so it was. I wolfed down an omelette.

Raimondo was also running a restaurant. He told his staff not to disturb us: he himself would be our waiter. He was very busy, on our behalf as well as with his business.

When he came by, I wanted to join the conversation. I told him, '*Mon père, il parle quatre langues*' ('My father speaks four languages'). It was true. Being fluent in four languages was partly why my father was a correspondent for Reuters, based in central Europe.

Raimondo smiled and nodded. 'Bravo. So do I.'

My mother gave a me look that meant 'Stop right there'. My father had revealed in his reports that Romania was increasingly succumbing to Nazi pressure. For this he was now on the run and our rule was to say nothing about him.

The military song and the boot stamping sometimes resounded close by. But here we felt safe. Raimondo brought us a fruit plate.

Eventually he brought our coats. 'Come with me slowly and wait just inside the door.' He exchanged hand signals with his cashier, positioned about halfway to our platform. Then he told us to go forward, slowly and purposefully. He also made an appeal. 'Italy is difficult now. Believe me, people here are sometimes good, sometimes misled.' He wished us luck. We thanked him.

Later, my mother said we should have wished him luck too. She worried that his kindness to people like us might land him in trouble.

Once I was installed in our train compartment, my mother visited the luggage van. She came back crying. Someone had slashed our suitcases with a sharp knife or a box-cutter. The hard leather hadn't been penetrated but the cloth coverings were in tatters. She explained later that she hadn't cried for the luggage, but for how the knife might have targeted *us*.

We made it to Nice. Was this a life-changer? Or just part of living and growing?

Physically, it helped us avoid interrogation, internment, being split up and possibly worse. But it influenced me mentally, too. I learnt that kindness exists in unexpected places; that languages are there to be used; and that my mother would have gone through hell for me ...

Once in a Lifetime

KAREN LETHLEAN

Marine biologists said it would only happen once, a phenomenon, swarming of bait fish off Cape Cuvier along the distant Western Australian coast. A desolate, rocky place, few got to observe the strange sights of an oil slick-like teeming with millions of anchovies, sardines or like tiny fish pushed in almost underneath cliff bases. Evening news carried footage along with noted experts attempting to theorize why.

Long forgotten when we took our road trip to Carnarvon, planned as an escape from Perth's wintery dullness; a chance to let in a little sunshine and spend time seeing unique things a ten-hour coach trip away. An outpost far away from the most isolated capital city in the world. Along highways with alien-looking termite mounds, some of them dressed — according to one source, 'more intelligent mounds wear shirts'.

Leaving suburbia early, watching dew dry on roadside grasses, over multiple cattle grids, where coach wheels thundered, through to passing a dark world, only a dotting white line visible beyond bus headlights. Arriving twelve hours later.

It was a coast touted as where desert and seashore meet. Touristy things like a visit to plantations fed by endless artesian reserves, pipes running into sandy expanses of the Carnarvon River, never a drop of surface river flow visible. Acreage given over to tropical fruits, mangoes and even experimentation with stone fruit. Produce driven the thousands of miles to Perth markets.

Wandering around town strengthened the sensation of having missed the town's heyday as a major export port. Defunct, unused for several decades, closed off since the mid-1960s. It was hard to imagine rails running out to One Mile Jetty pushing loads of local harvests to be loaded onto vessels. Yet out of the mangroves, expensive touring yacht masks appeared to grow. An alternative method to travel from the big city. Factoring in potential collisions with kangaroos on the highway, I still thought the coach was safer. Plenty of shipwrecks along this coast, including one famous for survivors still haunting the Abrolhos Islands.

'Be sure to bring your bathers,' the tour guide said when we booked our day trip, a chance to take in famous blow holes, which appeared to be a whale plume trapped under sharp rocks. 'There could be a chance to swim.' Hopefully not to become mashed tourists shooting skyward as a mist of blood and guts.

A drive out of town into shimmering salt lakes, and blinding yet appearing to be sky-blue coloured pools of water. Only when you came closer were mirages obvious.

I remember thinking how dusty, hot and isolated was this flat station land. How could anyone make a living out here? Known for feral camels released by earliest settlers, a location with little else than wild goats. When I worked for a meat exporting company, these beasts were caught, Halal slaughtered and sent to Middle East countries or sold for Easter. Little else was alive out here, until we swiftly pulled to a halt, burnt rubber smells still tangible in furnace-like air as we tumbled out of the truck.

'It's a Horned Lizard.'

A dust-coloured creature tried desperately to camouflage itself as a slight road bump, looking like a bonsai dragon with multiple horns upward in all directions. How on earth did our driver see such a tiny reptile? Two Japanese women were babbling and giggling. Soon enough the creature scampered away and we reloaded, by this stage longing for ocean. As if we are evolved life forms returning to cool blue depths.

'You can swim here; I'll park the truck for at least 40 minutes. But watch out for sharks over there.'

He pointed to visible dorsal fins that flipped and danced at the northern edge of what seemed a small, rocky reef. Swimming with sharks — a surprise day-trip inclusion.

Shallows, just beyond milk-white pristine sand, appeared heavy with seaweed drifting shoreward on gentle currents. As much as we craved a cooling dip in the ocean, this water didn't look so inviting.

'I'm not so keen to go in here, with all this weed.'

'Yep, doesn't look very inviting. What about over here? There is at least a bit of sand.'

We waded out into water so clear it was barely perceivable; warm too. Coloured like something touched by various artists. Azure, cobalt, cerulean, turquoise — words are insignificant as descriptions. No waves as an onshore breeze flattened everything perfectly level. We looked back at yellow, seemingly rust-stained cliffs surrounding this narrow beach, wondering aloud how this coast would change if developers got their hands on those ocean views. Conceding isolation proved beneficial; if all this were closer to population, like on east coast land, it would be Resort Ville by now. I was so glad hillocks there were not daubed with apartment blocks and wealth.

As we walked deeper, weed appeared to recede. With head under water, weed morphed into giant shoals of fish. As we swam they parted like shimmering, bejewelled curtains, making openings kindred to ever-changing undersea mazes which roll towards us. Swam in and fish encapsulated your every move. We couldn't see where these walls of fish began and ended, only that they were alive and moving. Tumbling over you couldn't perceive a sea floor, because swarming masses closed tight behind, above and under, forming a carpet of fish, and all about were finger-length bodies panicking to swim away from humans.

I reached out and tried to grab a handful, but all I could catch were a few scales and the sensation of live things slipping out of my hands.

Fingers are not made to hold sea creatures tight. A slight haze of oil was the only thing remaining on my fingertips. Half in and out of the water, it was possible to see fish jump just above surfaces trying to escape. As we stood in waist-deep water an adjacent ballet of dorsal fins took on a new meaning. The sharks were not bothered with us, because an all-you-can-eat buffet was right here. Their open mouths much more effective than human fingers at scooping up fish. Sharks cut swathes through masses, an aquatic feast trapped below towering shadow cliffs. Off to one side, we were just something forcing their quarry into eager jaws. A solo defence of hiding in a multitude doesn't feel effective.

Then we could see this black shape, which initially appeared to be seaweed, change and shape in an effort to protect itself, like a giant, single organism rather than millions of individuals. Predators were forcing the shoal in two journeys towards death; either into shallow shore waters, to be dumped in a high tide flotsam zone, or into jaws. Small fish swarmed about our legs as if we might be some form of security.

This became a point when I understood my own insignificance when faced with a lif-and-death situation. Along with a tumult of sensations to do with appreciating nature, relaxing in my own solitude, and trying to protect myself from life's predators.

Bear

KATE MARSHALL FLAHERTY

It was hard this morning, to figure what to do with all the food in a box on the porch. The days are still cold, so the cheese and eggs should be okay, but I feel restless, like a pacing beast, my heartbeat thick yet rapid. I found a single packet of yeast, and feel it is such a treasure I want to bake bread right away, to savour with melted butter, but I want to save it too, as leaven is so hard to find. A treasure of great price …

What stays with me most, after four days of nailing up railings and slip-proofing throw rugs with rubber webbing, of sweeping cement bits from the crumbling farmhouse steps and washing flooded silt off cellar wine bottles, after red raw hands from sanitizing door knobs and light switches with Clorox and rags, after trips to the only grocer with a mask and rubber gloves, the panic of an itch in the nose, and did I scratch? Making a haven for my 88-year-old parents, after the COVID cases in the home, is my utter preoccupation these days. It is full-time work, on top of virtual work, and fills my days and nights. We plan to bust them out as soon as their test results come — in the next week, negative, and off they go to the old farmhouse.

I am weary from worry, yet sleep like the dead. My dreams undulate between peaceful clean sweeps and basements to clean, a line of golden preserves in amber jars on a sill in the sunlight, a new staircase in the old farmhouse we somehow never saw, its bannister lit by a skylight, to glass cases and rubber piped hose, tubes and a sushing ventilator, sliding glass doors and hospital blue gowns and glasses and the snap of latex as a nurse says, 'Anything you need to say, before the plastic breath slides in?' Anaesthetic dreams and déjà vus and wills scribbled in a rush.

My brother says about the test results, 'Well, if they are positive, it's game over,' as simply as if he was saying the crocuses are spiking up again this spring. My sister, the baby, cries, and I breathe deep. My mom sits in fuzzy blue behind my dad on Zoom, leaning in and laughing at something behind us on the screen. Her hands in her lap, upward palms open, laced in prayer, she is at peace. Is this the dementia, or a wisdom we learn from our elders? A distilling in her, a settling into the situation with acceptance, non-attachment, her childlike-ness a gift to us all, but a worry.

What stays with me, after the satisfaction of a pantry stocked as best we could with basics, a few treats, the *essentials* — a word I reconsider constantly these days — the thing that lingers in a way that quickens my pulse and brights my spine, is the image of that yearling black bear, standing on his hind legs, sniffing the air with his licorice nose and tan suede snout. Looking right at us, paws dangling down, tip of snout, and his thick, dazzling, black pelt, rich with tiny sparkles from the sun. Thick, dark, diamond-dazzling. He saw me, sniffed me, stood dignified and languorous, curious, unafraid, both of us, electrified in this spring sighting. He must have eaten well, his black pelt tells me, and slept soundly all northern winter. What a sign, to see him, as I try to make a safe cave for my parents, now that COVID has cases in their retirement home.

He ambles back to the bush, not green yet but still damp with frost melt and patches of earthy snow. I still see him standing before me, 20 yards away, and recall the safe settling in my belly seeing this creature of the wild. What a contrast to the city spaces, where every jogger who pants from behind, closer than 6 feet, causes my frenzied leap out of the way. Or the biking family shouting spit-sounds as they whizzed round the corner, with no room for me to step away from the spray, the ice in my nape and rage at their thoughtlessness. How strange, in these corona times, I am more afraid of a tot on a trike, a super spreader unaware of her distance, than the closeness of a 900-pound bear, on his hinds, 6-inch claws dangling, sniffing my scent.

I can be a she-bear, *mukwa*, ripping the bark off in rage if someone tries to hurt my cubs. I can bat the air with sharp words, roar at wrongdoings, splinter the silence of injustice … and yet no one is to blame that there is COVID in the world. No one to blame but ourselves. We hid in a dark cave of unconsciousness to what we do to the Earth, to each other, the way the world has lifted profits over people. Anne

Michaels said once, it is horrible the things we humans do to each other ... and amazing what we do for each other. We have seen both in these challenging times. Protest signs to kill the weak, as well as re-think the rules; greed and hoarding as well as creative compassion across boundaries and borders. But here I preach. I think out loud. I go to my head.

I want to be like the bear, sniffing the scent of the moment, awakening from the dark place, from the cocoon, the hibernation from the world in a deep sleep, unconscious but breathing, dreaming, trusting in a little resurrection — the world different than it was when we entered the cave.

PART 3
MOMENTOUS DECISIONS

As soon as questions of will or decision or reason or choice of action arise, human science is at a loss.

Noam Chomsky

ɳ

This is the night
That either makes me or fordoes me quite.

William Shakespeare

A split-second decision can change the shape and direction of your life. Part or sometimes the whole of one's subsequent life can be traced back to the decision-making moment. Atim Onen's prize-winning story takes us to her discovering 'that moment on the run changed my life. I realize that I can use the moment that changed my life to change the life of others.' An eight-year-old Alanda Greene took a life-defining decision after family members on a boat trip disregarded her entreaties to save a life. Amal Abou-Eid, an Arabic-speaking Australian teacher, found a new purpose in life when she took someone's advice and became a playgroup mother. In an impossible family situation, Vanessa Shields made the astute decision to select hope rather than choose between conflicted positions. Kay Middlemiss knew and heard what she wanted and that was her turning point — but how was that decision taken? As Jillian Dagg was growing up she couldn't find the stories she wanted to read so she made the decision to become a writer and reports that 'not once have I regretted my life as a writer'. Isobel Stewart selected an international life seemingly in response to an advertisement for a job her husband could fill. And so a life changes direction and turns towards a different future.

Peace Club

ATIM ONEN

*Keeper of Indigenous Knowledge,
the Community Museum of Peace
of the African Child Soldier*

Sometimes what's best is what you cannot see, hear or feel. But when you have an ear to your story, a story that definitely reveals something about you, it is worth sharing. I have no idea where my life would be right now if I hadn't made a run out of it at that precarious moment.

My name is Atim, daughter of Onen of Patuda clan in Gulu District in Northern Uganda. My refugee mother gave birth to me in the bush and continued walking before the rebels could capture her. Atim means 'She who is born in the bush'. I lost both my parents in the conflicts between the government of Uganda and the Lord's Resistance Army led by Joseph Kony. I grew up hiding from the rebels who kidnapped children. They made boys into soldiers. They used girls for camp chores and as their bush-wives. It was a time when the nights were longer than usual. My dying father said he did not want me to remain here on this Earth to suffer. It was then arranged with my relatives that when he passed on, I would be taken to live with one of my aunts in Kampala. It was in 1998. Then in 2003 it was decided by the clan elders that I was becoming a woman and should be married.

Soon after, one dreadful day, my aunt got really ill and I was sent to buy some medicine. Her husband offered to give me a lift on his bicycle. On the way, he began to tell me that my aunt was going to die, which frightened me. Then he asked me if my monthly cycle had started. I said that I didn't know. He asked rather rudely how I could not know. Then he added that, later that evening, I should take his water for bathing and wait for him in the shelter near the house. I felt like I wanted to jump off from his bicycle and run far away from him. When I returned home, I told my aunt and my grandma what happened. To my astonishment, they both told me to just keep quiet and not tell anyone about it. I was puzzled and disappointed at their response. I refused to take the water for my uncle because something inside me was telling me that if I did, he was going to rape me. On learning that I didn't take the water for bathing, my sick aunt became furious and threatened to beat me, an ungrateful orphan, for being disobedient.

At that moment a word came into my mind that changed my life: run! I ran as fast as my legs could carry me, not knowing where I was going or the repercussions of disobeying the adults who had looked after me, an ungrateful orphan. I felt the energy that connected me to the universe vibrate in my body. My body began shaking but I kept running in the dark. I did not know where I was going. All I knew was that I wanted to run and be far away from my aunt and her husband.

My feet were burning. My body was exhausted. It was nearing dawn. I just collapsed by the roadside and waited. For what? For whom? I don't know but I waited and I waited. I was in shock. I did not cry or feel hungry as the sun rose and then it was nearing lunchtime. Suddenly, one of my distant relatives caught sight of me. She asked me why I was there. I tried to explain but the pain in my heart stopped my tongue. Words choked in my throat. Finally, I cried and I cried. She said she could not leave me there alone. I could come stay with her.

Some weeks later, my one of my great-aunts organized a meeting with the elders of my Patuda clan. They banished my uncle from coming to visit his wife. That was shameful in my culture. Such a man was ridiculed. Later, I heard he died of HIV/Aids. I could have been the victim of that incurable disease if I had lost that moment when I ran that changed my life and submitted to my uncle's lust because of my obligation to my aunt, his wife, who fed me, an orphan.

When I visited my great-aunt to thank her, she was very happy that I came. She lived alone. She asked me if I could read and write. I said yes, I had taught myself. Right away, without waiting another minute, she called out to a gentleman passing by and asked him to take me to the nearby primary school to get enrolled. At school, I actively participated in clubs. One of the clubs that best related to my life's journey was called Peace Club, because it was my intention to save girl children orphaned by war and all others who were broken because of conflicts.

Peace Club is the reason I am the woman I am today. My life's journey through the Peace Club did not end there. I met many more wonderful people like Cecilie, the Norwegian lady who heard my story and sponsored me to do a degree in anthropology at Makerere University in Kampala. I met Dr Sultan Somjee, an ethnographer, who has turned out to be my mentor and who awakened my inner self. I wanted to go back to study Indigenous knowledge, what we call Utu in Swahili, or Ubuntu as they say in South Africa. It is the same reason why I am writing now. I wanted to study that because I saw the wisdom and justice in the elders' judgement on my case, in the old way, when the modern society including my own educated people have become corrupt and immoral. Dr Somjee started coaching me to develop my interest in Indigenous African peace traditions. I am working on it now. I have excelled and even published an article. He then made me the Keeper of Indigenous Knowledge at the Community Museum of Peace of the African Child Soldier so I can use my trauma to help others. This responsibility of working for peace among the conflicted Acholi of Northern Uganda and Southern Sudan is my goal in life and a healing journey of many losses. I wouldn't have achieved all this if I hadn't run away from my caregivers. By running away from my relatives, I screamed out a loud alarm. I can now speak with courage and tell our people, especially men and my relatives, to look at themselves in the mirror and see what they do to orphaned girls during wars. It was that moment when I ran, and I ran, and I ran, up to today I don't know where to, but I ran. That moment on the run changed my life. I realize that I can use the moment that changed my life to change the lives of others too.

Choosing sides

ALANDA GREENE

The afternoon gave no hint that it would shape the rest of my life. How could I possibly know it would, just eight years old with no idea how one's life can change in a moment?

My mom and dad, two older brothers, my grandfather and I were together on a rented boat southwest of Vancouver Island. My grandparents had recently moved to Victoria and that summer our family had driven from Calgary for our first visit to their new home. To go fishing in the ocean had been my grandpa's long-time dream; my parents were happy to help the plan along; the kids were along for the adventure. None of us had sailed on ocean water before.

The water's dark green, like the shadows of the trees thick along the shore, remains a vivid memory still, as do the huge grey cliffs and the thick scent of salt water. It was brand new to a prairie girl who had known the smell of water as the crisp tang of creeks, known air that was dry and trees that grew hardy and small, unlike these coastal giants. Jellyfish floated by like small girls' chiffon dresses, water slapped the shoreline boulders, gulls circled against the blue sky, whining complaints. I was enthralled with this newness and hung over the boat's rail while my mother chatted with her father. She sat beside him at the end of the boat where he held a thick, light brown fishing rod over the white V lines of our wake. Dad steered at the wheel and moved us slowly, chug chug chug, along the coastline. My brothers watched, tousled and pointed out an eagle perched on a bare branch.

Suddenly Grandpa called out and great excitement ensued. All of us scrambled close to watch as his rod arched, then relaxed, arched again. He was thrilled. 'I've got a fish. I think it's big.' Over and over he wound the reel while the pole bent in a steep arc, then released the handle to rapidly spin the opposite way. I looked to my father quizzically. 'He's tiring the fish so it won't break the line,' he explained. 'Pretty soon he'll be able to scoop it up with the net.' All of us caught the excitement, waiting for a glimpse.

Then it came, the splashing of white foam and the flick of a silver tail as the fish surfaced and dove again out of sight. 'It's ready,' my dad said to Grandpa. 'I'll hold the rod if you want to net it.'

My grandfather nodded, handed my father the rod and took the net hanging on the inside edge of the rail. I leaned over as far as I could to watch as he scooped the net under the surfacing fish and lifted it, thrashing and twisting and spraying cold drops over my face.

Grandpa hoisted his catch and swung the net with both hands over the rail and across the boat, where he dumped the dark grey fish into a rectangular box near the opposite side. The box was painted pale blue like the floor of the boat, nothing at all like the deep green where the fish had been. My grandfather grinned as wide a grin as I'd ever seen him grin. Both my parents grinned too, happy for him. My brothers giggled with excitement.

I stood frozen in horror as the fish, a sea bass, continued to flip, arch, smash its tail, its side heaving, eye wide, mouth gaping. 'Oh, please,' I wailed. 'Let it go. It's hurting.'

The others looked at me with amazement and some amusement too. 'We can't let it go,' my dad said. 'Grandpa caught it. He's so happy. That's why we're out here.'

'But it wants to live. It's dying. It's in pain.' Couldn't they see this? I was sobbing now and the fish was getting weaker. My brothers laughed and made fun, my parents tried to console me and explained how the fish had to die, that this is what happens.

But I was inconsolable. I tried to convince my grandfather but he was getting irritated with me. No one was interested in my pleading and instead were praising Grandpa for catching such a fine fish and landing it so well.

I realized, in a moment of helplessness and horror, that this beautiful fish would not be given its life and its freedom. It would die in that box of air. My throat burned, my heart ached and pounded in my chest, and tears drained in silence. I looked at these people I was with on the boat and they seemed to be strangers and not my family. I looked at the fish, its sides heaving up and down, every so often trying to thrash its body back to water, to escape what appeared to me as agony. Its great round eye gazed at the blue above. I sat down on the boat floor beside the holding tank where it lay in its death throes.

Softly, I apologized. For my grandfather, my parents, my brothers — their uncaring action. I apologized for me, that I could not convince these strangers to let the fish go back to its home, that I was helpless to save it. And I promised I would remember it always.

In that moment, I also made a promise to myself. I will not be one of them. My allegiance will not be to people. People kill these beautiful creatures for nothing more than pleasure. I will be on the side of the creatures. I looked squarely in the eye of the dying fish and I chose my side. I may have looked like these other people but I made a solemn promise. 'I will not be one of them.'

Playgroup

AMAL ABOU-EID

'You'd probably benefit from attending playgroup,' said the maternal child health nurse. Her name escapes me, but those words never will. It was then, in the depths of post-natal depression and anxiety, that I reached out for help. I was sinking and gasping for air. Help me, I pleaded with her. I need to connect. I feel alone. I feel isolated. Playgroup was her solution. I was desperate.

A few weeks later I became a 'playgroup mum' — attach to that title what you will. I walked in nervously, husband by my side. I couldn't do it alone. I wasn't ready to take two children out on my own just yet. The first session went well. I reconnected with my eldest. Or tried to. We played a little, laughed a little and sang some nursery rhymes. The newborn slept. The whole time! *This will be fun*, I thought. And it was fun, for the most part. Yet there was still loneliness, there was still isolation. I was different. I wore a headscarf on my head. My son's name is Khaled. 'What does that even mean? How do you pronounce it? It's probably best to stay away. She probably doesn't even speak English.' Sometimes, looking away can be just as hurtful as staring. We were ignored. We didn't make any friends. We didn't belong there. Yet we didn't stop going.

It was fortunate the facilitator didn't share these sentiments. She always spoke to us. She always greeted us by our names. She made us feel good. She gave us a space to play and to smile and to belong. She was doing her job. She did it well.

Months rolled on and another set of impactful words, this time from the playgroup facilitator. 'Would you consider becoming a playgroup facilitator? We can't seem to crack the Arabic community. Mothers often come for one session and never return ...' *I wonder why*, I thought to myself. 'And, well, you're bilingual and they might respond better to someone like themselves.' No surprise there. We often feel more comfortable with people who are 'like' us.

But I'm a high school teacher, I thought. I teach English and history, my students can read and write and sit at their desks. That's what I'm good at. That's what I *want* to do. Yet it was a good opportunity. I couldn't go back to teaching any time soon. Juggling two kids and a career was out of the question. This was as close to education as I could get at that moment in my life. It was close to home, it paid well and I would have some time away from being Mum a few hours a week.

I needed them and they needed me. Why wouldn't I say yes!? It gave me a chance to give back, to feel useful again.

I accepted the job. I became a playgroup facilitator for the Arabic-speaking community and later for a multicultural/multilingual group as well. I worked hard. I enjoyed it. For a while. Until one day, I was told the laws and rules had changed and I was deemed underqualified. More life-changing words. 'Complete a diploma in early childhood education and you'll be right,' they said. So, I did. I registered. I bought the textbooks, new pens and highlighters. I started an online course. I hated every minute of it. I hated the course content. I hated the modules, the assessments and the quizzes. I hated the research and the hours of scrolling through PowerPoint presentations and YouTube videos showing me how to change a nappy and how to swaddle a baby. I knew all of that; I had two babies of my own! Yet there I was. Enrolled in a course I hated, to keep a job I no longer wanted.

Somewhere along the road, in the haze of that year, I attended a local publisher's book fest at a library. I watched on as author after author sat in front of the children and read their stories. They stayed on afterwards to sell and sign copies of their books. It ignited a spark. I wanted to do that. I wanted to write and read and meet and greet. I recalled the vice principal at my old school. How boring everyone thought he was. Not me. I barely listened to *what* he said, but I was always mesmerised by *how* he said it. Motivational speaking. I wanted to do that. Inspire the youth. Shake them out of their apathetic state. I could barely get my children into a proper routine. Forget writing. Forget speeches and guest appearances, your baby is crying.

But it was at that time, while enrolled in that course, that I found my calling. It was one particular PowerPoint presentation that spoke directly to my purpose. The importance of belonging, being and becoming, and linking a child to the world around them. The presentation explained how a child is linked to family, community, culture and place. I learnt this concept at the same time as being asked questions from my son's kindergarten teacher. 'Why do you wear that? What happens during Ramadan? How often do you pray?' and on and on and on. I love answering questions about my faith and my culture. Knowledge is important. We never stop learning. So I answered all her questions with vigour and enthusiasm. We were often the last ones to leave the centre. I had so much to share!

As an educator, I valued the importance of reading and literature. As a mother, I wanted my children to be able to access books that represented them and their lives. Books that taught them morals and values. Books that had characters who looked like them, spoke like them and celebrated like them. I wanted books that answered the questions I was asked. I wanted a book that was for Arab Australian children. I wanted a book that represented me, that reflected my family and me. I wanted a book that would link my children to their identity. I couldn't find it. But I wanted it. So I wrote it.

I had wanted to write a book when I was eighteen years old. The scribbles. The drafts. The notes. They sat there hidden away in a journal somewhere in my garage. Everything I had gone through in that year all led up to that moment. *I* will write the book. *I* will become an author. *But wait*, I thought, *hang on a second. I'm not a writer. I don't know how to write and publish and sell and promote and … what else do authors do?*

Wrong. I am, I can and I did. I met my publisher, I pitched my idea and, less than one year later, I held a copy of my first children's book in my hand. A book that has sold over 1000 copies and counting. A book that has been read around the world to children from different faiths and cultures and customs. And it was all made possible because my maternal child health nurse believed 'playgroup will do me good' — and a lot of good it did me.

An epic love story

VANESSA SHIELDS

We kept the last chair closest to the aisle in the front row reserved for my father. Though he told me that he would not attend my wedding, my heart held hope that he would change his mind and show up.

My husband and I got married on a hot, sticky day in July on a stage in our favourite theatre. Lovers of film, we created our wedding day celebration like it was a film premiere — complete with 35 mm film draped over vintage film canisters, a movie poster for a wedding invitation and red carpet under our feet. Our love was an epic romance; a real tear-jerker and completely Oscar-worthy. But as it happens in filmmaking, the behind-the-scenes realities told different stories than what was presented on the silver screen.

My relationship with my father was tumultuous in our first act. We were a misguided and misunderstood father–daughter duo who couldn't seem to find a common storyline. It didn't help that my father and mother were married at nineteen then divorced by 21. The drama between my mother and father was electric, shocking and motivated by an anger subtext that lasted decades. I was a kid caught up in a drama I neither created nor understood until I was in my teens. Cue the inciting incident.

```
INT. OFFICE — DAY
A fifteen-year-old girl calls her father on the
phone.
```

```
                    DAUGHTER
              Dad? It's me.
```

```
                    FATHER
              I know.
```

```
                    DAUGHTER
         I have something to ask you.
```

```
                    FATHER
              Okay. Ask me …
```

DAUGHTER

Remember when you said …

In a flurry of courage and curiosity, I grilled my dad on details about things he'd said and done in an attempt to create my own narrative about his life, about his choices. He answered every question without hesitation. My heart expanded and opened a room just for him. We laughed. We cried. We let the old story go and committed to a 'call to adventure' worthy of an epic hero's journey for each of us. Cue the montage.

INT. KITCHEN — DAY
A daughter hugs her father.

EXT. PARK — DUSK
A daughter and father sit on swings, gently moving forward and back. The father throws his head back in laughter.

INT. CAR — NIGHT
A daughter and father sing along to an Elvis song.

EXT. DRIVEWAY — DAWN
A daughter waves to her father from inside her car as she pulls out of the driveway at his house.

For years we rewrote, edited, revised and rediscovered each other. My father loved Elvis. My father loved grass so much he made a golf green on his front lawn. My father loved hockey something fierce. My father was a comedian. My father was an inventor. My father had dreams. My father felt stress. My father wasn't speaking to his siblings. My father … was a flawed hero.

The deal was that if I wanted to see my father, *I'd* have to *go see him*. He would not come to see me. Where I lived … was a closet of skeletons too numerous, too disheartening to face. And so I did it. I went to him. I took trains. I drove cars. I made him a construction-paper, art-and-craft book about 'me'. If the moment when I handed it to him was a hashtag it would have been #overwhelmedbutgrateful.

The deal was that loving my father had conditions. I understood that when I was old enough to understand that. But I didn't know that his conditions were so … concrete. So when the wedding invitations went out and I didn't get a response, cue The Ordeal.

```
INT. KITCHEN — AFTERNOON
A daughter calls her father on the phone.


                  DAUGHTER
            Hi, Dad. It's me.


                   FATHER
             I know.


                  DAUGHTER
        Did you get my wedding invitation, Dad?
```

FATHER

Yes.

DAUGHTER

Can you make it? I'd really love for you to be there.

FATHER

You see, I can't go.

DAUGHTER

What do you mean?

FATHER

Did you invite my family? Your aunts? Cousins?

DAUGHTER

Of course.

FATHER

Well, if they go, I don't go.

DAUGHTER

(beat)

I don't understand.

FATHER

I won't be in the same room as my family.

DAUGHTER

But it's my wedding. It's important to me that my
father, that *you* are there.

FATHER

I'm sorry, but I'm not going.

I remember hanging up and telling my soon-to-be husband that my father wasn't coming to our wedding. I remember he embraced me as I sobbed and snotted onto his shirt shoulder. I felt #confusedsadbroken. I felt our epic journey, our duo-hero adventure crumbling onto the cutting room floor. Were we finished before 'wrap' was even called?

That moment changed me. I had a choice to make. And after that choice, many more choices that could make or break my relationship with my father. I chose hope.

We kept the last chair closest to the aisle in the front row of the theatre I was married in reserved for my father. Though he told me that he would not attend my wedding, my heart held hope that he would change his mind and show up. He did not show up. But after we were pronounced husband and wife, I pointed to that chair from the stage, and I thanked everyone who joined us in celebration of our love … and everyone who did not.

The fourth threshold in the hero's journey is freedom to live. It follows the catharsis and the resurrection. It follows atonement and, in my case, forgiveness. It is an ending that incorporates a new beginning. I went to visit my dad after my wedding. I showed him photos of our red-carpet, love story wedding 'premiere'. He was #movedtotears.

The moments we miss carve holes into our centres. But these holes are refillable. Two years into my marriage, my father died of a massive heart attack. At his funeral, the church spilled out mourners onto the street. A friend sang an Elvis song in front of the altar. Eulogies flowed like water to wine. The loss was devastating. Still is. But we have the freedom to live a hero's journey, in all its fabulously flawed glory. And freedom to live means freedom to love. #amomentcanchangealife #love

I have been waiting...

KAY MIDDLEMISS

'Look, there's the house!' Tom swung the car off the country lane and parked in front of a pair of rusting, wrought-iron gates. 'What did I tell you? It's falling down. It had to be for that price. When an estate agent says it's been empty for some time, what he really means is it's ripe for demolition.'

We had been looking for the right house for such a long time. I was certain I did not want to step into someone else's dream home. 'Something that needs a little work, as long as that's reflected in the price,' had been our mantra. Neither of us had been to the Isle of Anglesey before but house hunting can become a way of life.

We stared out of the car window at the dilapidated building half-hidden behind a wilderness of hazel and goat-willow. My husband saw missing slates from the roof, peeling plaster, damp walls, cracked windowpanes and a lot of work to make it habitable.

I saw an ancient stone church with an empty belltower; a place built almost two centuries ago from local stone by craftsmen without the help of modern tools. It had been a place of refuge where farmers and countryfolk would come to ask for help and give thanks for a good harvest. A place built with love. 'It's beautiful.'

'It probably was, once,' he conceded. 'But what a strange place to build a church. It's miles from anywhere.'

'And it was a church, not a chapel, which is unusual in Welsh-speaking parts,' I added. 'I wonder what happened to the bell?'

'They have to remove them when churches are de-consecrated. That was over twenty years ago, according to the agent. They can't take down the tower because it has a preservation order on it.'

'You wouldn't take down the bell tower! It would be sacrilege.'

'Well, that's not our problem.' Tom reached for the pile of For Sale brochures on the back seat. 'Where to next?'

'No, wait. We've got the key. I want to look inside first.'

'You're not thinking ...?'

'Oh no. I only want to look.'

While Tom sat in the car and thumbed through the brochures, I turned the huge iron key in the lock, pushed open a door that was rotting at its base — and stepped into another century. Spiders' webs festooned the hallway where lines of green and grey damp climbed the walls. Was this the set for a horror movie?

Instinctively I turned and walked into a shadowy space that had once been filled with light and sound, happiness and sorrow. Chiselled oak beams rose from the quarry-tiled floor to meet beneath the apex of a slate roof. Seven Gothic windows filtered pale sunlight through the overhanging trees outside, and through a missing pane of glass came a gentle bleating of sheep and the far-off mew of a buzzard. The smell was not of incense but of dust and decay, and air that had been too long in one place. Silence lay heavy on the empty space no longer filled with rows of pews. Once, people had prayed here for their hopes and dreams to be fulfilled; had asked for the forgiveness of their sins and for the comfort of others in distress.

Do buildings have a voice? I don't mean the moans and groans of ancient timber and stone. Nor am I imagining ghostly whispering or creaking doors. But does all that energy left behind by human emotion sometimes find a way of conveying itself in near-human terms? The only way I can describe my feelings at that moment is to say, 'the house spoke to me'.

'I have been waiting for you for a long, long time.'

Tom was not to be convinced. 'You haven't even looked at the rest of the house,' he said. 'The extension is as big as the original church and it's got five bedrooms, according to the specs. Why on earth would we need five bedrooms — unless you're thinking of running a B&B?'

'I hadn't, until you mentioned it. Let's take a look.'

The builder had taken advantage of the full height to make a two-storey extension but with little imagination. A wide passageway gave access to a row of small, square utility rooms. I walked its length, tapping on walls to find which were load bearing. 'This one can come down; knock these two rooms into one; patio doors and maybe a conservatory on the south-facing wall ... And this could be my study.' I felt the green-mildewed walls of the small room wrap themselves around me in a comforting way. 'Yes, I could write here. This is somewhere I could finish my book.'

'Stop, right there! We are not even thinking of buying this house. It would take every penny we have and the rest of our lives to turn it into your dream home.'

'What else are you planning for the rest of your life?'

In the end, of course, we compromised. Tom agreed to make what he called a 'silly offer'.

'Oh, he won't take that,' the estate agent was adamant. 'It's already been reduced. I'll ask him, of course, but he won't go down any more. Now, let me show you this lovely bungalow. It's just come on the market.'

As the tarmac stretched ahead, leading us further and further from the rugged mountains and quiet valleys of North Wales, a gloomy silence filled the car. While the flat fields of middle England gave way to London suburbs, I gazed out at rows of identical semi-detached houses, each with its rectangular garden and carpark drive and I knew that this was not where I wanted to spend the rest of my life. As we rolled past Heathrow Airport, where I would be turning up for work the next morning, I realized that travel had finally lost its glamour.

'I'm sorry,' said Tom as we parked outside our own suburban semi. 'Something will turn up one day.'

'Nothing will be quite like that, but I suppose you're right. It would have been a massive task but such an adventure ...'

'I know, maybe I was rather hasty.' Stepping into the familiar hall, Tom reached past me to answer the ringing telephone. 'Probably a shift change,' he grimaced. 'Welcome back to the real world.'

Suddenly I saw him tense. 'Yes, speaking. What!' He put his hand over the telephone and turned to me. 'You'll never believe this. We've just bought a house — on Anglesey!'

It all seems such a long time ago now. We employed a local builder and a year later moved into our new property. There has never been enough time to finish the book, but I have had some success as a short story writer. An enthusiastic writing group meet at the house and once more the rooms resound with joy and friendship, and hope for the future.

One day I shall walk into my beautiful room with its tall windows turned away from the night sky, and in the warmth of the wood-burning stove I shall take up my pen and write that final chapter.

I chose the writing career

JILLIAN DAGG

There are many events that shape an existence. Although not many that alter the entire remainder of the lifespan to exactly match the desired outcome.

I was born in England at the end of World War II. As there weren't many toys in those days, books were my gifts. I still have some of them. I was very young when I was reading. And I loved reading. But as I grew older I found the stories weren't exactly the type of stories I wanted to read, so I wrote my own.

I moved to Canada with my parents when I was fourteen. I wrote all the time in my school notebooks. Short stories that I could write *the end* to. Mostly romantic stories. I didn't think of publication in those days; I don't think I even knew it was possible. I just loved reading and writing. I loved paper, I loved pens. I took a commercial course to learn to type. And my father bought me a portable typewriter for home.

I got married, moved to England for a few years. I met someone who wrote for Granada TV and I was told that I could actually get my stories published. I bought my first writers' publishers directory. By now I had read tons of romance novels. I had written about three short romances that had been rejected as not for that market.

I packed up those manuscripts and returned to Canada to live. I worked in offices. I kept on writing. In the hot, humid summer of 1977 in Ontario I had a small portable typewriter, a pile of canary yellow newsprint and I typed the title *Rain Lady*. My idea was about Marisa, an actress married to a famous screenwriter, who had gone into hiding because of her suspected infidelity. In keeping with the romance plots of the day, Marisa had escaped from California back to Canada where she was born. She was now living in Toronto, fearful that one day Lewellyn Stone would seek her out. And he did. He approached her agent with a manuscript, a new movie, *Rain Lady*. As she was broke, she was forced to accept the deal.

Now I had the title, and a vague idea, I needed to write the book; 50,000 words was the standard for a romance. Eventually, about a year later, out of a pile of cut-and-paste newsprint I finally typed up an original manuscript on a rented electric typewriter.

There were few romance markets but Harlequin Toronto was the main one. Not for us, they said. Too literary. Not discouraged, I saw an advertisement in *Writer's Digest* magazine for a new romance line. Silhouette Romance, Simon & Schuster, New York. I sent them a note, asking what they needed to see. They asked me to send the manuscript to them. I did. In the meantime, I'd written another book called *A Race for Love* about an injured racing driver and a marriage of convenience, always a popular romance theme then. I'd also sent that to Silhouette.

I was working full-time as an administrative assistant at an art gallery in December 1979. After a rushed day I came home, cooked dinner and prepared for a drive to a local college for a creative writing course I was taking. When I began writing there were no courses. I'd taught myself to write fiction by reading, writing volumes of words and studying books by my favourite authors. As well as articles and books about writing. Attending creative writing was a way to call myself a real writer and legitimize what I was spending all my spare time doing. My main writing day was Sunday afternoon. It's difficult watching everyone outside enjoying themselves on a sunny day when you're indoors immersed in a fictional world. Yet I did it because I had to. I had no choice. The stories wouldn't stop coming so they needed to be written down.

I was ready to leave the house for my course when the phone rang. An editor. Simon & Schuster, New York. The editor was lovely. I'll never forget her. She said they would send a contract. Could I come up with a pseudonym in the next day or two?

I don't recall much after that. I drove the dark highway to the college in a dream. I'm sure the car tyres were 3 feet off the road. I think I walked into the class and told everyone right away. The teacher was a wonderful man. He was a writers' magazine editor and had published a small piece of mine recently, *Can I Call Myself a Writer*. Now I could.

My head buzzed from smiles and congratulations. *I'd sold a book. A whole book.* I was 35. And I became Faye Wildman writing for Silhouette Books.

I returned to my job at the art gallery and life went on, interspersed with conversations with New York editors. I got into an elevator with a work mate who said to me, 'So, you're published with Simon & Schuster, New York,' and everyone stared.

A few weeks later I sold my second book, *A Race for Love*. I had no revisions on *Rain Lady* but needed to add a scene to *A Race for Love* to make up the required word count. I did all this while still working. And it was typewriters and snail mail in those days, so I had to allow for delivery by the very short deadline I was given to deliver the manuscript revision. My first experience with deadlines.

However, I had to come down from the delirium for a while and make a decision. Should I stay working and write in weekends and spare time as I'd been doing all my life? Or should I quit the job, take the plunge and write full-time?

It's not been easy. Publishers, editors and trends come and go. I didn't know it but I was on the cusp of a huge transformation in the romance genre. My older type of plots began to stop selling. However, I had always wanted to write more of a modern romance anyway. My first three had been turned down for that reason.

Gradually, through the years I've sold many more novels. I can't stop writing. It's part of me. I wrote when I was a child and now into my senior years. The muse doesn't stop. Did I make the right decision back in 1980? Yes. I've met tons of other writers. I've been to conferences that have allowed me to travel and have learnt way more about the craft. Not once have I regretted living my life as a writer.

A Life-changing moment

ISOBEL STEWART

A simple advert was all it took to change my life forever.

I was content living in Scotland with husband and one-year-old son but deep within my soul burned a wanderlust to see and do much more with my life. A wanderlust inherited from my ancestors who had trekked many lands and sailed the high seas.

I was flicking through a local newspaper when an advert caught my eye: 'Engineers and teachers required to work in South Africa. Jobs and houses provided. All transport costs, visas and work permits covered.'

'The answer to my prayers,' I whispered, then I picked up my son and danced around the room. He giggled as I sang, 'Paul, we are going to see elephants, lions and giraffes.'

The minute my husband returned from work, I pulled him into the lounge and declared, 'We are going to live in South Africa.'

'What are you talking about?' he spluttered, then I showed him the advert.

'We can't just up-sticks and head off into the wild. We have a beautiful home, a child to consider and a very comfortable life here. Have you lost your mind?'

However, I would not be put off. South Africa was all I could speak about for days and in the end my husband agreed to phone the company.

Two weeks later we were on our way to London for an interview and returned home having both been offered jobs — my husband as an engineer in the steel works and myself in an English-speaking school. We had another two weeks to make our decision.

'Wasn't it wonderful?' I said all the way home. 'The houses looked lovely, no job to look for, all expenses paid. We could rent out our house here, go on a three-year contract and if we didn't like it could come home again. Just think of it as an extended holiday.'

'We will see,' was all that he said, but I knew him too well and saw he was excited too.

Six months later, I had my own way when work permits and visas arrived. We were all packed up, ready to begin our new adventure.

Leaving family and friends was more difficult than I had imagined, but once on the plane I knew we had made the right decision and couldn't wait to settle in our new homeland. I wondered if this was how the pilgrim fathers felt as they left for the long journey to America.

I was ecstatic, the searing heat of the sun raining down on my back as we walked to the car that would transport us to our new lives.

Schools had just begun their summer holidays, so I had plenty of time to settle into our beautiful new bungalow, hire a housemaid and make friends. My husband, on the other hand, had only a few days off to help with picking our most important purchase — a comfortable new car. This was the way I was going to explore as much of this country as possible.

Every morning, I would rise with the sun beaming down from a cloudless sky and set off to see places of interest in the area, never regretting for one minute the choice I had made.

I learnt a lot about the history of the country and began to understand the cultural differences between the tribes of the land. Sometimes my housemaid would astound me with her beliefs, such as the day she asked for four bricks and some newspaper. I could not comprehend why she should want them so watched as she wrapped the bricks in newspaper, set them out on her bedroom floor then rested her bed on top of them.

'Now!' she declared. 'The Tokoloshi can't get me as I sleep. They are smaller than a brick and don't like newspaper.' This was her way of making sure that she would not be taken away by the night spirits.

The one thing that bothered me about South Africa at that time was the apartheid system where black people were not accepted as equals in the eyes of whites. However, although we could not change the system, we could treat the people we met with courtesy regardless of colour or creed, and my husband and his friend were the first white people to play semi-professional football for a black African team.

Life soon settled into a routine of working during the week then setting off on a Friday evening to discover more exciting parts of this wonderful country we now called home. We had to be careful we did not travel too far as petrol stations all closed from Friday evening till Monday morning, and for that reason cars always carried extra cans of petrol in the boot.

The time I loved most of all was when friends or relatives came to visit, and we could take them on holiday. Those were the times when we discovered places such as the historic Kimberley Diamond Mine, the beauty of Cape Province, the stunning Garden Route, Durban and the Valley of a Thousand Hills.

South Africa exceeded all my expectations in so many ways.

Seven years down the line, after exploring every corner of this spectacular land, I saw another advert. 'Engineers and teachers required to join a new diamond mine opening in the Kalahari Desert of Botswana.'

But that is another story.

PART 4
TRAGEDY LEADS TO CHANGE

The tragedy of life is often not in our failure, but rather in our complacency; not in our doing too much, but rather in our doing too little; not in our living above our ability, but rather in our living below our capacities.

Benjamin E. Mays

4

This world is a comedy to those that think, a tragedy to those that feel.

Horace Walpole

4

There is a saying in Tibetan, 'Tragedy should be utilized as a source of strength.' No matter what sort of difficulties, how painful experience is, if we lose our hope, that's our real disaster.

The fourteenth Dalai Lama

4

I can't go on, I'll go on.

Samuel Beckett

*U*nanticipated, sudden and grim events are often the axis upon which lives are fully changed. While tragedy is part of the human condition, the writers here demonstrate that so too is the ability to learn from it.

Vaughan Rapatahana writes a powerful inspiring piece on how he purposely rebuilt his life after the moment that a familiar person rang: 'His news was that my son was dead. He had hung himself a few days before.' A serious maritime accident in Vancouver led to an inquest, the process of which led seaman Tony Smith to becoming a barrister. Children's author Dimity Powell learnt, when on a working Greek island holiday, a very hard way to forever 'accept the fragility of perfection'. Sixteen-year-old Gayle Malloy experienced sadness at the sudden death of a new friend and 'realized that any moment could be the last for someone. I must strive to never take anyone for granted again.' But as Blanche Morrison eloquently ends her poignant story, 'With all its pain, loss and broken dreams, it is still a marvellous world.'

Whakataukī

VAUGHAN RAPATAHANA

When the telephone rang one Monday evening in October 2005, it was the moment that changed my life completely, and without warning.

I was staying at the home of friends because the head office for my job was in Gisborne and my own home was way up on the east coast of New Zealand's North Island. I could not travel back there every day.

I had earlier that evening been reading the *Gisborne Herald* and on the inside front page was a small item about Wellington police seeking any information on the identity of a young man whose body had been found late in the previous week. I thought no more about this piece — until the telephone call …

On the other end of the line was the partner of my ex-wife. He sounded upset and shaky.

His news was that my son was dead.

He had hung himself a few days before.

It transpired that my son had disappeared from his Wainuiomata home and his wife had rung his mother — my ex-wife — and she and her partner had flown to Wellington to help find him. When they reported his disappearance to the local police, they learnt about the young man's body being found in Cannon's Creek, Wellington.

He was 29. Happily married, as far as I know. In his own home. My wife and I had travelled to see him several months previously and all had seemed fine, although I had not had much to do with him since. I should have made more effort to ring him.

Thus, the life-changing telephone call, which immediately whirled me into a tailspin of shock, then later into a series of mental squalls, whereby feelings of guilt and spasms of anxiety and depression ransacked me for a considerable time.

For about a year or two afterwards, I acted oddly. I abruptly altered course in key life decisions pertaining to relationships and jobs. I was erratic, restless, sad. I often broke into tears unexpectedly. I found myself brooding all too often. My own mental equilibrium was out of kilter.

Now, fifteen years later I still feel the pain. Still cannot expunge the often-recurring thoughts about my son and all the what-ifs about his demise. I find myself still writing poems trying to assuage the loss, the grief, the self-examination about what I could and should have done to prevent the needless suicide.

That telephone call, then, altered me considerably, across several zones. It was but a brief synapse in time, a moment, but its reverberations have shimmied ceaselessly across the lake of my own existence.

Initially, I researched and learnt a great deal more about the dreadful disease called depression — which had also affected me severely back in my own distant past. My son had, on reflection, been suffering from its ravages for a considerable amount of time. Yet, such is its cunning, depression does not necessarily send manifest signals to observers that its victim has become afflicted.

More, I became far less intransigent about others, most especially those who had issues with their own health, both mental and physical. In other words, I became less selfish, although others may not think I have done so. But I do believe that I have far more compassion.

Accordingly, I am nowadays far less materialistic. Less bothered by owning stuff, possessing things that I probably never needed in the first place and which are not living, breathing items of humanity.

And I am certainly more thankful for the natural beauty of my everyday surroundings, the native bush, the sheer verdancy of vegetation. I listen to bird calls in the morning. I am often near rapture when I see a swan glide gracefully across the lake in my hometown. We thoroughly appreciate the mercurial character of our pet dog.

That phone call, that moment where I learnt about the demise of my son, totally revised my life goals, expectations and priorities. I retired just as soon as I could; not interested in pursuing any career, nor chasing massive fiscal sums. Became more focused on enjoying life with my wife and whānau. Very appreciative of even having this koha, this gift of life, in the first place.

Ultimately, then, I more fully embraced my own ancestry, found solace in being Māori. In so doing, I made a spiritual voyage from one doomy whakataukī to more positive ones. From tiwhatiwha te pō, tiwhatiwha te ao (gloom and sorrow prevail, day and night); through ka heke te roimata me te hūpē, ka ea te mate (when tears and mucus fall, death is avenged); to he oranga ngākau, he pikinga waiora (positive feelings within you enhance wellbeing).

The sad irony is that this tragedy led me to become a far more complete person.

If only it had not come at such a great cost.

Sailing towards the Bar

A.C. SMITH

'The accident's a blur, yet you're adamant that before leaving home the headlight was on. How can it be?'

'Because my father lost his legs on a motorbike ...'

Mine was the palpable sigh when the jury's verdict excused the infraction. My mentor would never have blundered into that even had it been *his* first case.

On a sweltering 1972 November day between my sea-going examinations, an engineer suffocated when carbon dioxide discharged into the engine room of a ship moored in Brisbane, Australia. How the fire retardant escaped would become the subject of an inquest.

Nearly a year later, the twinkling coastal lights beckoned my dream of visiting America. I was third engineer on the M.V. *Erawan* and we tied up at Long Beach. I wandered *Queen Mary*'s holystoned decks, Anaheim's sprawling Disneyland and Universal Studios' backlots, earning a Kojak-style grin from Telly Savalas before we steamed north to Tacoma. There Mount Baker loomed, its frosty peak jutting above swathes of cloud, my first vision of snow.

Vancouver BC lay ahead of a beatific afternoon's passage through Puget Sound. It was the most stunning coalescence of land and sea I'd ever navigated, teeming with fish, dolphins, birds and all manner of aquatic life inviting this red-ribboned, black cigar of metal into their playground. Would that our companions' gymnastics during their marine convocation throughout my deckchair-lazing never end. Only the deepening dark forced its curtailment in deference to midnight duty.

The *Erawan*'s stentorian engine required compressed air to manoeuvre it during docking. An elongated pressure tank suspended 3 yards above the controls facing me on floor-plate level served this function. At 3.15 a.m. the telegraph from the bridge was rung to 'standby', necessitating a reduction in revolutions. The junior engineer was beside me, as protocols demanded, and he started to wind back the governor. At the instant I opened the air valve, three things occurred: a distinct bump, an unquenchable blast of air and a signal to 'stop engines'.

Searching in vain for the split seam in the tank, my eyes captured a telltale spewing from the CO_2 pipeline. The Brisbane fatality flashed across my mind. All had to evacuate with alacrity, and it was so ordered. Three fugitives, scrambling up endless steel stairs for our lives, magnified the silence when the generators shut down and blackness fell like a thick blanket. Whipping out a torch, I made for the bridge. The bow of another ship was wedged into ours for'ard of the crew's accommodation. I buttonholed the second mate. 'What do you want me to do?'

'Put on your life jacket and say a prayer.'

I fled to my cabin and attended to each. In another instant he was behind me. 'The chief and second are down below.'

'What?' I cried. 'The place has been flooded with carbon dioxide, not ocean.'

As we approached the access point, the chief engineer staggered into the companionway, gasping for breath and managing to report, 'Graeme's trapped'.

Kicking apart the lugs of the great steel door and peering into the eerie gloom, my torch lit upon our man slumped on one of the ladders. Oxygen tanks were procured and the second mate was soon kitted out like a deep-sea diver. Instinctively, I put on a smoke helmet, adjuring the Chinese crewmen to pump air for me, their quandary apparent as to whether congregating at the stern might be preferable.

Hardly giving a thought to what we were doing, we plunged into the gaseous milieu and, between us, manhandled the 17-stone Englishman aloft to the open deck where he was laid out. I chose mouth-to-nose resuscitation and his breathing emerged stronger. The first words he offered on regaining consciousness: 'I thought that bastard,' signifying me, 'had buggered up the job.'

'Why did you go down when everything was dark?' I asked.

The chief's reply was statesmanlike. 'We needed to assess whether the engine room was taking water. I realized when we neared the plates that there was no oxygen and turned around, telling the second that we had to leave.'

As daylight approached, we were surrounded by a flotilla of tugs, slick-lickers and curious craft. The two ships were pulled apart, revealing that one of our fuel tanks had been punctured. Two hundred tons of heavy oil had escaped into the harbour, leaving a sizeable slick being contained by booms. Under Victoria Island's picturesque purview, we were wallowing several nautical miles from landfall.

Despite having taken on copious quantities of sea water, we stayed afloat. The other vessel was Japanese-flagged and of roughly the same tonnage as ours. The *Sun Diamond*'s bow had been peeled open like a tin of salmon but she managed to limp back to port under arrest, as did the *Erawan*, with the notices proclaiming admiralty detention affixed to each foremast.

A couple of days later, we were towed into dry dock for repairs. On being informed that it was the second release of carbon dioxide in little more than an equivalent number of months, the first having extinguished an engine room fire in Bangkok before my tenure began, I concluded the ship was jinxed and wanted to pack my bags. But before that instinct produced a resignation letter, all changed. First, the chief tasked *me*, rather than the second, with the job of assessing how much steel would be required to effect repairs and I was introduced to a Vancouver attorney, Mr Cunningham.

Tall, rangy and middle-aged, a handsome thatch of hair neatly parted bore out an intuition that here was a man whose disposition would be as equable as his appearance. There wasn't a scintilla of information respecting the events of that night about which he feigned interest. I obliged by making a comprehensive statement. Absent gloves and still attired in his immaculate, pin-striped business suit, having declined the offer of overalls he insisted on an expansive tour of the engine room.

No notes were made but it was clear from his questions that he took everything in as if his grey head secreted an indwelling microchip. Back on deck, seeming to relish the grease he'd acquired, there was grudging acceptance of a cloth.

'Just one more question out of interest more than relevance: what was it that led you to evacuate so quickly?'

'It goes back a ways.'

In another week the action shifted to the only occasion where Mr Cunningham's eyes bore the exuberance out of mine.

'Just remember to tell the truth and nothing can touch you.'

When came my call as a witness in the taking of evidence before the British Columbia Superior Court, I felt as if he could have made a seamless transition to my berth for the voyage back to the Far East.

Following the pre-hearing and gushing like a schoolboy, when he complimented my presentation, I canvassed a career in law.

He replied in a jaunty Canadian twang, 'Well, why don't you go and do it then, son?'

And so, almost nine years later, bewigged and gowned, I rose to be admitted to the Queensland Bar, a path presented by a moment that changed my life and managed to save it, too.

Kismet's odyssey

DIMITY POWELL

'Where is she? Where's Dim? Oh God ... '

Thump. Thump. Thump. The relentless, jarring drumming of a shovel thrust onto the top of a coffin.

Argh ... Just leave me alone to die. Please. I made a silent vow to never mix Metaxa and Retsina again. The hangovers were brutal.

Thump. Thump.

I staggered out of my semi-conscious stupor to the door, wincing with the effort of being vertical, wondering if I had missed the carpool to work.

'You're here?' *A matter of opinion.* Brad, my British boss stared at me as though I was an apparition from Hell. A cluster of my workmates, the lead crew couples, jostled in the cramped doorway behind him.

'We thought you were with him.'

Be careful here, Dim. You need this summer job, I cautioned myself through a fog of confusion and lack of sleep. 'Um, with who?'

'How did you get home last night?'

'I got a lift back from the marina,' I replied, grateful my 'lift' had not lingered and I was alone in my apartment, except for the anxious-faced thrum of people in front of me. 'Why? What's going on?'

Brad sagged against the doorjamb, misery pooling in his eyes. 'It's Mickey. He's gone.'

'Gone?'

He sighed painfully as though his whole body was deflating. 'Mickey's dead.'

Single vehicle. Accident. Blind drunk. Transit van. Write-off. Greek hospital. No chance.

Fragments of explanation slewed around an otherwise funereal soup of silence like chunks of putrid cabbage in the back of the transit van; Brad upfront, driving, the rest of us stuffed in the back, inert and mirthless.

Don't look up, don't look. I kept my head down, slumping deeper into shock as we travelled along the same stretch of road where just hours before, Mickey's van, the one he was supposed to take me home in, had concertinaed itself into a traffic light pole.

By the time we clambered out into the uncompromising Corfu morning light of Gouvia Marina, my hangover had metamorphosed into a brick of disbelief lodging itself in the pit of my gut, raw and hard. I crawled aboard the nearest Jeanneau. In the last few months, this sleepy seaside village's population had swollen from its usual handful of battle-scarred street strays and tired taverna proprietors to an eclectic community of casual workers and tour operators. In another week or so, the Brits would arrive, ready to embark on their Ionian sailing odysseys but there were still cabins to detail and engines to service before the charter season began in earnest.

I began scrubbing the decks, attacking each tattoo of rust with numbing ferocity until it disappeared in a slurry of deck wash. How dare they blight this ship's exterior with their imperfectness. Didn't they care how hard we'd worked on these vessels? We were young and already hopelessly seduced by the briny island breezes that bounced across the Ionian Sea. Invincible and more deeply bronzed than Odysseus himself. Perfect, like Mickey.

Younger than any of us, taller than Zeus and almost as strong, Mickey was our gentle giant with a smile longer than a yardarm; always there to help and heave. A kid housed in an Olympian's body.

Lost. Too young. The Fates leave nothing to chance. Almost Easter. His poor mother. It could have been me…

Known as a 'top-shelf' girl in this part of Kontokali and thus favoured by the bar owners because of my preference for imported spirits (stored on the topmost shelves), I was a foreigner with waist-length hair and a sunny air of semi-permanency who knew half the Greek alphabet and at least six other Greek words and never turned down the offer of a drink. In short, I was good for business.

But I'd spent most of last night tucked away in George's, Kontokali's local pita grill, with Brad, Mickey and the lead crew. George replenished our table with bottles of Retsina as though it was Perrier. We'd celebrated with gusto; the fleet was almost ready to set sail, each flotilla booked to the gunwales. It felt good to relax after weeks of antifouling hulls and re-rigging masts.

'Your motorbike arrives next week,' announced Brad.

What?

'It'll make meeting-and-greeting our charterers so much easier,' he added brightly.

'But I can't drive a motorbike,' I'd protested. Or did you ride a bike? I had never even sat on one.

'Don't worry! It's easy,' he promised.

I'd rather negotiate the Bermuda Triangle on a toothpick than navigate the streets of Corfu, at night, alone, on a motorbike. Fortunately, the Retsina had dissolved most of my stomach lining so I couldn't fully feel the awful grip of dread taking hold. Curse shore-based job descriptions.

'Sure,' I agreed reaching for one last soggy chip before we spilled out onto the street.

'Now make sure you get a lift home with Mickey,' said Frank, speaking to me but looking at Mickey like a father on prom night. I was the lead crew's soft spot. Mikey gave them a reassuring nod before we parted ways. Drawing on my confident familiarity with Kontokali's olive-scented twists and turns, I soon found a favourite haunt to dilute the turpentine aftertaste of Retsina and didn't see Mickey again until the witching hour had been and gone.

By that time every club resembled the same soulless cavern, filled with obscure slurring spectres and annoying four-to-the-floor rhythms. I was ready for home. And then, there he was, ridiculously dwarfed by

Mickey's lumbering bulk, staring straight at me, the reason I'd hung about for so long. Ever since Brad had ordered he 'Get off the quay!' a couple of days ago, I'd been yearning to gaze into his sea-glass green eyes again. A right lad, this boy was, full of cheek and party, only his sombre expression suggested tonight wasn't a party night.

'It's late,' he shouted above the thrumming crowd. 'Come on, I'll take you home.'

'Mickey's taking me,' I stammered through an indignant tangle of rising disappointment and anger. Why was he acting so … *sober*? 'Aren't you, Mickey?'

We'd both peered up at Mickey. He grinned stupidly back at us, an Amstel clutched in each hand, swaying slightly like a giant redwood moments before it's felled.

'He can't,' my self-appointed knight insisted. 'Mickey, give us your keys.' But Mickey was beyond words, let alone rational thought. Mickey and I stared at each other in a trance of drunken resignation. 'Come on,' he said again reaching for me. 'I'm not drunk. I never drink when I've got a cold.'

Without asking again, we left; left Mickey staring into nothingness with his Amstel and a whole life ahead of him.

It could have been me …

I watched the boy on the moped approach. He wasn't welcome on this part of the quay but Brad wasn't around to lecture as he pulled up centimetres from where I stood, staring at me with those green eyes.

Realization tore through me like a chilling Albanian katabatic wind ripping my breath away. *You saved my life.*

A silence as dense as quicksand enveloped the marina, neither of us able to find within it the words to acknowledge the hugeness of that moment. We stared, sinking, until finally, I whispered …

'Thank you.'

The pageant

BLANCHE MORRISON

We are all shaped by our past. The first few years leave the deepest impression, which will stay with us always. When we are older, we tend to go back to our childhood memories. It is like a wandering child returning home, a sort of solace amidst the crushing years. I recall this event, which took place many years ago. It is a memory of a child's special day now buried in the mists of time. I was unaware then, but what happened on that day changed my life forever.

It was the summer of 1936 and I was a happy, carefree child of seven years. The city I lived in was about to put on a show called a pageant. It was a sort of historical play performed in the open air. It usually took place in a large meadow before thousands of spectators and was really an amazing affair. It was a celebration of some anniversary connected with our city. The planning was done a long time in advance and it must have required expert organization. Every school in the city had to play their part and there was an air of great excitement at the thought of taking part in this most talked-about event. We chatted and giggled about it, with flushed cheeks and eyes like saucers.

One morning the teacher showed us a lilac-coloured material. This was to be made into our costumes. She let us run our hands over its soft and silky surface. The silver trimmings were most eye-catching. The teacher did her best to calm us down as we were so excited.

We were measured for our dresses and the teacher explained what was expected of us. We were so eager and lively and there was much childish laughter. For a few weeks we had to practise our parts. The teacher escorted us to the meadow which was about 15 minutes' walk from school. The grass was long and I could see butterflies hovering among different flowers of every shade and hue. There seemed to be scores of children standing about. Numbers were pinned to our backs in large print and then we all had to join hands and skip onto the field. We seemed to be pulled in all directions until we got it just right for the big day. Eventually we learnt where our positions would be. It was essential that we each knew our own place.

The noise was deafening, people shouting, whistles blowing. Some of us covered our ears to shut out the clamour. How our arms and legs ached! It was almost too much for us as the youngest competitors. There were many falls and a few tears, but much comfort was received from a dozen helping hands and so the tears were soon forgotten.

Each time we went to practise on the meadow, I noticed the many workmen hard at work sawing and hammering. They were building stands to accommodate spectators. I still recall that smell of new wood and even now its pleasant fragrance takes me back to that time so long ago.

At last, the day we were all looking forward to arrived. Everyone proceeded to school as usual in their ordinary clothes. We then changed into the pretty dresses that had been made for us. Some mothers were helping their children but mine could not be there as she was ill in hospital. I was very young at the time so accepted the situation, but how closely the past shadows us. Memory teems and sharpens. We never really forget 'the days that are no more'.

We marched in lines to the meadow with our teachers on either side. We must have looked the picture of innocence, little angels dressed in lilac and silver. We didn't act in the play itself but children from every year joined in an opening display. We knew exactly what to do, dancing on to the field, performing to the music. All around there was bright music and laughing voices and a sea of faces looking down upon us.

There were hundreds of children and each school had a different costume. The colours were really spectacular. As the youngest, we were called 'sunbeams'. I think to call us little rays of sunshine was quite appropriate. I can remember feeling the heat of the sun on my back and the smell of newly mown grass in my nostrils.

After we had finished our display we were allowed to sit on the grass and watch the play. Adults played all the parts with the exception of a few older children, who acted as pages. The actors wore period costumes. Some of them were sitting on horses — to me they seemed like giants with very loud voices. The horses were beginning to feel the heat. Their coats shone in the sun. They were becoming restless, disturbed by the music and loud voices.

Some of us decided to walk around and investigate the large tents on another part of the field. This was where the actors prepared themselves. I looked inside one of the tents and it was full of strange costumes and people getting ready for their performances. There seemed to be lots of nuns about and tall soldiers in unfamiliar uniforms. A man appeared with a cloak about his shoulders and a gold crown. It was all quite fascinating. I felt that we were all taking part in a fantasy and for a moment reality was suspended.

I did not have any idea of time at all, but some of us were beginning to feel weary so decided to make our way home. The hill on the way back was steep. I was glad it was downhill. My legs were tired, and I was thirsty and hungry, but even so it had all been very exciting. It felt like the end of a perfect day.

The shadows were growing longer now, and the air was cooler, but there was still a cloudless blue sky. As we walked down the hill, I was surprised to see in the distance my brother approaching. He was about thirteen years old but to me he seemed grown up. He was meeting me to tell me that my mother had died. It had happened while I was at the pageant. Lost in my daydreams I was oblivious to the situation. Many times since then, a childhood memory has been sharpened and the heart burns with unshed tears.

I was too young to really understand but felt sad and confused. My brother took my hand and we went home. I did not realize the impact this incident would have on my life. Nothing would ever be the same again, but then of course that is another story.

Later it was not a good existence, but one small human being survived against all odds and darkness does not go on forever. We all grow up, and ahead was a huge spectrum of experience waiting to be savoured. With all its pain, loss and broken dreams, it is still a marvellous world.

Echoes

GAYLE MALLOY

He had an understated masculinity to him. Tall and lanky with a playful grin, he looked at me, the creases at the corners of his eyes promising the warmth of a budding friendship. He was one year older, working, and therefore a man of the world. His name was Michael.

The year was 1969. Neil Armstrong had walked on the moon, the war still raged in Vietnam, and a festival at Woodstock had given young people the opportunity to escape into music for three full days. Everything big and exciting was happening somewhere else. I lived in the time-warp of Western Australia. If there was a counterculture, I had not seen it. Where I lived, there were no big music festivals or colourful hippies, not even a protest. At sixteen my life was humdrum and small.

The one flicker of excitement that broke the monotony of school and home was Friday night attendance at youth group. Students from my all-girls high school would gather in the cellar of the local church, listen to music and hope that someone's brother or a new teenage boy would attend. Life was simple. Although we were chaperoned, we still managed to slip away, hungry for the sweet taste of freedom.

Michael walked over to where I was sitting, plonked himself down beside me and whispered in my ear.

'I'm Michael. Want to come outside and have a drive of my car?'

'Can my friends come too?' I blurted out, delighted at the prospect of escaping the youth group and finally doing something interesting.

He studied my face, a hint of laughter on his lips. Nodding, he passed me his car keys. They felt wonderfully heavy in my palm. Perhaps they were the entrance to something new and exciting. Jingling them to get my friends' attention, I put my finger to my lips and motioned towards the door. Once outside, my gaggle of friends resumed their noisy chatter as they followed us to his car. It was light blue, old and battered, and the car seats sprouted foam where the leather had split. Giggling nervously, they squeezed into the back seat, five bottoms squashed into the space for three.

'You do know how to drive?' he asked.

'Of course,' I lied.

With the ignition on, I ground the gears into submission, placed them into first and the car jerked forward. Our adventure had begun. My friends shrieked with laughter as I drove his car slowly down the road, crunching gears and careening up kerbs. Michael was silent, patiently watching as I lurched down the road, the car now a cacophony of hysterical female voices. Finally, with my speed and the gear no longer compatible, the car came to a shuddering halt.

'Oops, I think I stalled it. Shall I start it up again?'

Michael's laughter bubbled up, childlike and free.

'Better give it a rest. I don't think the transmission can take another gear change. Let's swap seats and I'll take it from here.'

I gazed at his profile in the darkness of the car as he drove back to the youth group. Shaking his head, he was laughing quietly to himself, the noisy chatter from the back seat drowning out any possibility of conversation.

As my friends scrambled out of the car and hurried back to the cellar, I turned to him. His eyes were twinkling with joy as he studied my face.

'That was great.'

'Yes, yes it was,' he laughed.

Climbing out of the car, I was careful not to slam the door. No one likes a door slammer. Bending down I gave him a smile and a quick wave. He waved back, then slowly drove away. As I walked to the cellar, I realized that in my naivety I had sabotaged the opportunity to get to know him. Perhaps next time he would stay and talk. I wondered if he liked me.

The weekend was filled with mundane chores, homework and watching television. Monday's local paper held a small article on the front page. It reported the tragic death of a young man who had been working on his car. He had been under the car with the front wheels jacked up when the jacks failed and the car came crashing down on top of him. He was killed instantly. The photograph in the paper was of Michael.

There he was, smiling back at me, the Michael who had laughed good naturedly at my terrible driving. That Michael was no more. His laughter lines would never deepen with age, making him more attractive as his hair turned to grey. His gentle patience would never be shared with his children as he watched them grow to adulthood. His hopes and his dreams would never be fulfilled. He was gone.

The sadness that washed over me, seeping deep into my being, slowly turned to regret as I looked down at his smiling face. He had been kind to me and in the excitement of driving his car I had not bothered to thank him. It would have taken but a moment.

'Thank you, Michael. No one has ever trusted me with their car before. Thanks for being so patient with me.'

Three sentences. That was all it would have taken to let him know that I appreciated him and his kindness towards me. The sadness had been bearable but the regret was sharp, a rapier of pain. He had entered my life with the vibrancy and promise of new beginnings and now, three days later, all that was left was the finality of death. I had taken it for granted that I would see him again. At sixteen, for the first time, I realized that any moment could be the last for someone. I must strive to never take anyone for granted ever again.

The echoes of that day have accompanied me throughout my life. My world had been tiny and inward looking, but with Michael's death it expanded to include others. It took courage to speak, for there is always the risk of rejection. But over the years I have discovered that simple words, spoken from the heart, can pierce the most stubborn of barriers.

'You know you're important to me, don't you? Thank you for being a part of my life.'

I will always be grateful to Michael both for his brief presence on that day and for the deep learning he gave me. Whenever I see a tall lanky teenager with a gentle smile, he reminds me of him. The model of car that Michael drove is long gone, but for a while whenever I saw a car like his I would smile and remember the way he looked at me, his eyes twinkling with joy.

It was one day in a lifetime, yet the echoes of that moment are with me always. I am old now and my 'use-by' date is fast approaching. I hope that when I leave this life, I will be able to seek him out and thank him for the moment that changed my life.

PART 5
VIVID MOMENTS

Clarity is the hardest thing of all.

Julian Barnes

Unless you made your life a turning point,
there was no reason for existing.

Saul Bellow

The turning point in the process of growing
up is when you discover the core of strength
within you that survives all hurt.

Max Lerner

Do not dwell in the past, do not dream of the future;
concentrate the mind on the present moment.

Buddha

Do you not know that in a race all the runners run, but
only one receives the prize? So run that you may obtain it.

Corinthians 9:24

*I*n all lives, even those that are unexamined, there are moments of such power and clarity that recalling them readily demonstrates their seminal nature.

Bettina Deda's massage at a Kahuna centre in Australia's Byron Bay awakened her to the fact that 'one could tell the most memorable story in a conversation without words'. Rosaleen Kavanagh noticed that her parents' soft Tipperary accents were not suitable for enunciating a particular word in a conventional English way and this became a symbol of the way of the family. As a child, Glenne Findon was deeply mesmerized by a family picture of a beautiful lady in a blue dress; only when her uncle was dying was Glenne told that the picture was of her mother, who had died in childbirth. As a newly independent young man, Ryan Gibbs had a cat foisted upon him who taught him about adapting and living with others. A day with family laughter and trickery on a beach brings a warm memory of Madeleine Gill's much-loved and sadly missed uncle. Joy M. Mawby vividly remembers the finer details of the moment her childhood was changed by the news of her father's death. Diana Duckworth took a bus on her own at three years old and learnt to 'just buy a ticket'. Deborah Huff-Horwood remembers finding a fairy and bringing tears of joy to her grandmother. Finally, Diane Sims recalls the two words she used to take control of her life in a fraught situation.

A conversation without words

BETTINA DEDA

'Thanks for the dance,' Jay smiled at me.

I knew I would need to get up, put on my robe and slippers and leave this place where I had just experienced the most wonderful massage. Two days ago, I didn't even know what Kahuna meant; now I could still feel his fingers, wrists and forearms all over my body. Over 90 minutes, Jay had touched my heart and soul in a way that no one else had ever done before. And I did not want to believe that it was all over. Let alone think of the next morning when I would return with my husband to our life in Sydney.

It was 31 December 2016, and what was supposed to be a week of rest and relaxation in my favourite wellness retreat in the hinterland of Byron Bay turned into a series of unsettling events culminating in a 90-minute dance that turned my world upside down.

'The main difference to other massages is that Kahuna comes from the heart,' Jay explained at the beginning of my treatment while his right hand touched his heart. 'If your mind is as busy as mine, the best thing is to relax. My hands will be all over your body while I am moving around the table. This is my altar,' he smiled and touched the massage bed. 'I will listen and talk to your goddess; and she will tell me what to do.'

I tried to digest what I had just heard.

'I will start with your back, your legs and arms and then ask you to turn around to massage your head, face and the front of your body, your chest, belly, arms and legs,' he said as he explained the Hawaiian massage style further. 'If you feel uncomfortable with anything I do, please let me know at any time. I'll leave you to get ready and be back shortly.'

I took off my clothes, climbed on the massage table face down, and covered my back with the sarong he had prepared for me. Not long after, Jay returned.

He changed the music to a more rhythmic beat. I felt the sarong being lifted from my back. He placed a towel over my bottom and tucked it between my legs. He lifted my legs slightly and moved them apart so that my knees touched the edges of the massage bed. I felt the warm oil on my skin, his hands, forearms and elbows moving over my lower back making their way to my upper back, my arms and hands. After a while, I gave up thinking about where he was and what he was doing and completely surrendered to the rhythm of the music and the feeling that his skin on my skin aroused in me. I felt uplifted and grounded at the same time. At some point, he asked me to turn around, and the massage continued on my head and face.

'Bettina, are you happy for me to massage your chest?' While he was touching my shoulders with both hands, I could hear his voice very close to my ear and wave of heat ran through my body. Without opening my eyes and mouth, all I could articulate was 'Mm' before I succumbed again to this spiritual dance he had seduced me into.

He slowly lifted the sarong from my upper body. His hands touched my chest to slide down between my breasts to my belly and up again. The same dance he had performed on my back was now unfolding on the front of my body. I had completely lost any sense of time and enjoyed every second in this otherworldly wonderland of passion and compassion. In rhythmic movements, he followed the form of my body from my feet up my legs over my belly around my breasts towards my arms and fingertips — triggering feelings of surrender, vulnerability and happiness.

I again felt a deep level of trust and connection to this man I hardly knew. He seemed to answer my unspoken words with his hands and body, connecting from his heart to mine, talking to me without words. An experience beyond anything else I had ever encountered. By no means did I want this dance to end.

But then, his movements stopped. He covered me with the sarong and held me still with one hand under my head and one hand under my sacrum. I lay still, floating in a sea of kindness, compassion and love; in this moment, I knew that I would never forget this man, who now seemed to know my body better than anyone else.

Eventually, he lightly pressed his palms on my head, chest, belly, knees and feet and finished with touching my navel area. Then I felt a refreshing toner on my face.

'It is time to wake up and come back to the room,' his soft voice reminded me of the end of my treatment.

I slowly opened my eyes, reluctantly, resisting, not wanting to leave this wonderful place I had just discovered. What had he done to make me feel so comfortable, hardly talking at all? How had he got access to my innermost self, as if we had known each other for years?

Had I opened Pandora's box?

'Take your time, I will meet you outside.' Jay slightly touched my forearm, smiling at me once again.

When he finally served me a beautifully decorated tray with tea and fruit, he kneeled beside my chair and asked how I felt. 'Peaceful' was all I could think of. I found it hard to articulate any words. He explained that Kahuna massages can leave people with extreme reactions from crying to feeling utterly excited and that it was important to rest afterwards. Then he said goodbye and disappeared in the spa to attend to his next guest.

I kept sitting for almost an hour in the tropical outdoor space, trying to make sense of what had just happened. The only thing I could see with total clarity was that something in my life was going to change. I savoured the lemongrass tea and the fresh fruit. The bite-sized pieces of papaya, orange, melon and grapes tasted so much better than the days before. I still felt as if I was floating in an infinite ocean of love.

I didn't want to share with anyone what had happened. I wanted to keep it in my heart, cherishing that one could tell the most memorable story in a conversation without words.

Threepenny bit

ROSALEEN KAVANAGH

I became aware of the significance of the missing letter H as soon as I started school aged five, in a small town in the south of England. It was 1962.

In the evenings, after our meal, I would sit on my mum's knee at the small Formica table and play the game I had invented, 'Say what I say'.

'It's *three*pence Mum, that's how everyone here says it.'

'*Tru*ppence,' my mother laughed at herself in her soft Tipperary accent.

'Put your tongue between your teeth Mum,' I encouraged. 'It's *three*pence.'

When it was my turn to copy Mum, I would stumble over strange Gaelic phrases she remembered, 'Dun do bheal'.

Dad, also from Tipperary, wasn't much better at mastering the TH. He looked like Paul Newman, it was said. Black hair, chiselled face and searching blue eyes.

I was born in Belfast in 1957, at the height of the Troubles, when Dad was working at a huge aircraft factory in the city. Dressed in his supervisor's coat, white shirt and black tie, he would stand with his clipboard beside big turbo plane engines.

Dad was responsible for quality control, signing off repaired engines as being safe.

'Do it again,' he would instruct one of the blue boiler-suited men. 'That measurement should be *tree tousand*, not two.'

'You can't see the wood for the *trees*,' one of the men invariably quipped.

'Do it again,' said Dad. 'I'll be back to check it.' He would turn his back to ripples of laughter.

Even that white supervisor's coat couldn't protect him from the mockery of the aircraftsmen. When Dad's mental health began to decline, and my mother could no longer tolerate the bricks through the window, a transfer request was signed by the doctor. We crossed the sea to England, my six-month-old self oblivious to the rough seas and the puking breaths of my three elder siblings. But the Troubles had spread to England and terrorist bomb blasts punctuated my childhood.

Dad said little about his new job at an aircraft yard, but it involved him inspecting helicopters with dentist-like mirrors for tiny cracks the apprentices might have missed. His strained expression when he came home from work was constant. He muttered about the eejits who could not understand him.

I wondered why I could perfectly understand my parents' broad Irish accents but had to translate what they were saying to my friends. From the moment I realized my parents would never master the TH, my campaign to fit in evolved.

I got a part-time job in the local library to fund after-school speech and elocution classes with Mrs Blake. She was an eccentric old lady with straggly grey hair who lived in a large, decaying house on the posh side of town. The other pupils, mostly girls, arrived in their school uniforms of straw boater hats and grey badged blazers. I would rush home from the local comprehensive school to change out of my second-hand uniform before catching the bus for my lesson. One of the other girls would usually open the door, before joining her friends in a tight ringed circle. I began to realize how Dad must have felt at work and was relieved that my drama teacher had wobbly shelves of dusty classical books for me to peruse while I waited for my class to start. Mrs Blake would often give me extra lesson for free. I was trained to walk across her airy, wooden-floored studio with heavy books poised delicately on my head. Sometimes she would have me lie on the floor and do deep breathing exercises. When I had to wear a tooth brace for months, the troublesome sibilant 's' sound was soon dealt with.

Mrs Blake entered me for elocution exams and local competitions. My favourite performance piece was Eliza Doolittle from *Pygmalion*.

'What's that you are rehearsing?' quizzed my mum when she heard me practising in the kitchen.

'The rain in Spain stays mainly in the plain,' I trilled in my best received pronunciation British accent.

'It's about a young girl,' I hesitated, 'who has to adapt how she talks to get on.'

Mum nodded and took an interim puff on her cigarette as she rolled out the pastry for the apple pie.

When the evening came for my first drama festival, Dad offered to take me in his bright green Ford Cortina. He wasn't familiar with the location, and we drove around dimly lit streets while I checked my watch and Dad cursed the lack of directions. When we eventually arrived at the hall, I strode up to the adjudicator's table in front of the stage, ignoring the hushed silence of the audience.

The judge turned to me in her elegant blue suit, hair in a perfect bun, and glanced at her watch. 'Just time for one more,' she said and gestured to the steps at the bottom of the stage.

Mum placed my trophy in the centre of the living room mantelpiece the next day and cut out the front-page article in the local newspaper: 'Lost Rosaleen shows the way.'

When I finished my degree in English and drama at university, my parents missed the award ceremony. Mum was not a driver and her map-reading had never been strong. They arrived in time for the garden party afterwards, though. Dad insisted on hiring an official photographer; Kodak instamatics were not good enough for the first graduate in the family. Trying not to teeter in my borrowed black stiletto shoes, I smiled in my buttoned-up blue blouse and black pencil skirt while the crinoline-suited photographer snapped away.

'Here you are,' said Dad, counting out the pound notes and coins when it was time to pay.

'What's this?' asked the man, holding up one of the coins, eyeing it suspiciously.

'It's *tru*ppence,' smiled Dad.

The photographer raised his eyebrows and looked at me.

'Dad, where did that come from?' I laughed, taking out my purse. 'Threepenny bits went out of circulation in 1971.'

The lady in the blue dress

GLENNE FINDON

The little girl stood there mesmerized. She looked up at the picture on the wall way above her head in her neighbour's house. It was a picture of the most beautiful lady she had ever seen. She had the most perfect face, endearing eyes and Mona Lisa smile. She was tall and slim and was wearing a blue dress that reached to the floor. It had intricate embroidery and beading on the bodice and a small train that was swept to the side. She wore a hat in the same blue colour, and it was trimmed with handmade roses. She carried a big bouquet of pink roses, dahlias and carnations. The little girl thought she was just like a princess and decided that one day she would like to look just like her.

The little girl grew up with her younger brother and sister, but she always felt different from the rest of the family. Her father was the ex-army sergeant-major type, with a stiff upper lip and strong principles. There was never any nonsense allowed in this family and success was expected rather than praised. She was much taller than the other members of the family and as she grew older, she noticed this striking difference. She was withdrawn and quiet, meek and mild, a quiet achiever and one who was seen but never heard. In comparison, her younger siblings were far more gregarious.

One day, when she was about twelve years old, the little girl's life as she knew it changed forever. She was skipping along the footpath opposite her house, when an old lady stopped her and uttered, 'Hello. You must be Betty's daughter.'

'No,' said the little girl. 'I am Beryl's daughter.'

'No,' said the lady. 'I am sure you are Betty Kelly's daughter.'

As she carried on her way, the little girl stopped in her tracks. Mr Kelly lived next door. So who was Betty Kelly? She had never heard of her, so decided to ask her father that night when he got home from work.

When her father was relaxing in his easy chair with a beer, she plucked up the courage to ask.

'Dad, the lady over the road told me I am Betty Kelly's daughter. How can I be? Who is Betty Kelly?' she asked innocently. The colour drained from his face. After a long silence, he said, 'She was your mother. She was Mr Kelly's sister and she died a long time ago. Now go to your room.'

The little girl was stunned. So Beryl wasn't her mother after all. No wonder she felt different to her siblings. And Mr Kelly must therefore be her uncle. From that moment on, she felt that her life as she knew it was a lie.

There were many questions she wanted to ask her father, but not being one to question his authority she carried on her life, too scared to bring up the subject again. She was also too afraid to ask her uncle. Despite knowing that the woman she called 'Mum' wasn't her birth mother, she tried to put this fact to the back of her mind. But she never forgot the mutterings of the old lady and her father's revelation that her birth mother had died. She couldn't understand why her father and uncle were so secretive about her mother.

Many years later, the girl's father died, so she visited her ageing uncle. 'Who was Betty?' she asked.

'Betty was my sister and your mother. She died ten days after you were born due to complications associated with childbirth,' he said.

The girl was shocked. Many questions followed about her mother, but her uncle was getting old and couldn't remember a lot of the details. However, he did recall that she was tall and elegant, and looked just like a film star. She was a dressmaker, always looked smart and made all her clothes including her wedding dress. She was very popular and always had lots of friends.

'She was a lovely person,' he said, as he gave his niece a small black and white photo of her mother to take home with her.

Ten years later, she was phoned by her uncle. He asked her to come and see him for a few days. She went immediately, as she knew he wasn't well. When she arrived, he got out a large box of photographs from a cupboard. Although she could see he was in pain, he insisted on going through them all. There were many photos of her mother — all black and white or sepia.

'Keep any that you want,' he said. 'I won't need them any more.'

They spent a whole afternoon together going through the box. When they had finished, he walked unsteadily to his bedroom and came out with a parcel.

'I have kept this especially for you,' he said. 'I remembered your grandmother saying that you always looked at this picture. She said you loved it, so now it is yours.'

She unwrapped the parcel and inside was the picture of the beautiful lady in the blue dress.

'That is your mother on her wedding day,' he said. They were both crying as she gave her uncle a big hug and thanked him for the beautiful picture of her mother.

The next morning, she was woken by the sound of voices. She got up and saw an ambulance in the driveway of her uncle's house. He was being carried out on a stretcher and they took him to the hospital.

That was the last time I saw my uncle. He died that night. Yes — I was the little girl in this story. Having never known my mother, and having had her memory excluded from my life for so long, was difficult to comprehend. Why didn't my father or uncle tell me about her? I later found out that my father had sworn the whole family to secrecy and told them they must never mention my mother to me. But why? Whatever his reason for not telling me, my father carried it to his grave. It made me sad that in all those years, I never knew anything about my mother and if I hadn't met the old lady from across the road on that fateful day, I still wouldn't have known she even existed.

The picture of my mother in her blue wedding dress has been on display in my house ever since. I just wish I had known more about her earlier in my life when people who knew her were still alive. Nevertheless, I am sure she is my guardian angel leading me along life's way. She certainly is my shining star — to me she is Venus, the goddess of love and the brightest star in the sky. I often look up at Venus in the night sky and think of her, just as I did as a little girl, when I looked up at the picture of the beautiful lady in the blue dress.

A case for Cassie

RYAN GIBBS

One day my aunt called to say that my uncle, a lumber contractor, had found a cat abandoned in the woods. He had taken pity on the animal and fed her pieces of his hotdog before carrying her out of the woods, cuddled inside his lumber jacket. My aunt stressed how much she had wanted to keep the orphan, but she already had a cat of her own, and so she offered the cat to me.

I wasn't sure I wanted a pet at the time. I was enjoying my first job away from home and had just picked out my first apartment. I was looking forward to my new-found independence and did not want to compromise it with the added responsibility of caring for a cat. But now it seemed I had little choice: take her in or face the guilt of knowing I had turned away an abandoned kitty. So I agreed to take her in

When my aunt dropped her off, I realized she was only a kitten, one year old. And although she was very thin she was by no means lethargic as she raced around the room, spinning across the hardwood floor and jumping up on the chairs. I had a hard time falling asleep that first night. There was a window above the bed, and the cat kept jumping from the bed to the window to the bed. She'd land on top of me like a wrestler delivering a body slam.

The morning came too soon as I awoke to find her resting on top of my head, purring loudly and licking my face to tell me it was time to wake up and feed her. When I finally got the food ready, I discovered I had mistakenly given her shredded cat food instead of the pâté she preferred. The cat refused to eat. I thought to myself, *it wasn't that long ago she was starving in the woods, and now, all of a sudden, she's so fussy?*

That night we both slept a little better. Although the cat still jumped around the room, she did manage to settle down for brief periods of rest. She preferred to sleep between my legs, which I didn't mind at first, but it soon felt as though I were lying on a torture rack with a block of wood between my ankles. When I moved onto my side, the cat curled up in the curve of my bent legs and fell asleep.

As the days passed, I tried to think up a name for the little tyke. I thought about her black and white coat and recalled the many black and white movies I used to watch with my grandmother before she died. I decided to name the cat Casablanca (Cassie for short).

The name seemed to fit her as she reminded me of my grandmother. Every time I got home from work, she was there to greet me. She would sit beside me on the couch and listen to how my day had gone. These talks were of great comfort as I became increasingly disheartened by the long hours and menial pay of part-time work — as long as Cassie was around, I was never talking to myself.

At last I got a full-time job and planned to move across the province. Cassie sat by patiently as I loaded up a rental car with everything I had, then placed her in her cat carrier and sat her in the front seat before setting off on the ten-hour drive. To my surprise, Cassie never cried during the trip; as long as she could see me, she was content. I had never known a cat to be such a good travelling companion.

Once we arrived in the new place, I set Cassie loose in the apartment and she treated it as an adventure: sniffing carpets and exploring closets. She disappeared until after I had unpacked and gone to bed. She then curled up in the curve of my bent legs and purred contentedly. I was amazed she had adapted so well; it gave me hope I could do the same.

When I arranged my first trip back home, I feared locking Cassie away in the apartment. I decided to ease the anxiety of the lengthy separation by asking one of my colleagues, Clarissa, to check on Cassie when I went up north. It was a difficult decision. Even though I felt comfort knowing the cat was cared for, the thought of someone entering my apartment when I was away seemed a violation of personal space. But in the end, Cassie's needs trumped my insecurities.

Unfortunately, I should have invited Clarissa over before I left. When she arrived at the apartment for the first time, she found a cat in the hallway and assumed it was mine. Only after she had let the animal inside did she realize that my cat was lying under the bed. Luckily, she managed to find the stray's owner without any incident. Despite the mix-up, she agreed to cat-sit whenever I went away, and I have since made the effort to have people over more often.

When they arrive, they can see how much influence my cat has had on my living room décor: the floor is littered with little plush toys and plastic mice. Even my effort to introduce plants into the apartment bears her mark. The potted trees are wrapped in tin foil to protect them from her claws, and the flowers are bent from her occasional naps inside the pots. I try to explain to Cassie that she needs to learn to live with others; it's a lesson I know she has taught me.

Derek Peddle

MADELEINE GILL

My toes wriggle impatiently in the sand as I look out to the sea.

'Come on Mads, get in! I promise, you won't even see one.'

Reluctantly, I crawl out from beneath my umbrella and shaded safety to stand up. The sun is burning hot, its rays piercing my fair skin.

They're in the water, bobbing up and down rhythmically as each wave passes. I see my mum and sister laying on the sand, turning like rotisserie chickens to ensure the sun tans every inch of their bodies. I honestly don't know how they do it.

Hot, hot, *hot*.

I skip across the sand as quickly as I can, my feet wincing with each step. I welcome the sudden cool of the sea as I reach the shore, the waves lapping around my ankles and the wet sand clinging to my toes.

'Get in!'

The menacing jellyfish warning sign lingers in the back of my mind as I step further forward. He's smiling at me, waving for me to swim out further. He promises that there are sandbanks for me to stand on, that he hasn't seen any jellyfish.

I'll do it, if it means I can spend time with him.

I lower my body in and swim out to where my uncle and brother are, saltwater stinging my eyes and lips. I really, *really* hate the sea.

'See? There was nothing to worry about,' my uncle says as he helps me to reach the sandbank. My feet gratefully touch the surface. 'Me and your brother haven't seen one since we've been in.'

He's lying, I know. I try my best to ignore the red jellyfish sting marks covering his arms and shoulders.

Forget the jellyfish.

We bob in the water for a little while, throwing a ball back and forth between us. After about 20 minutes or so I decide to swim back to shore, keen to get back to my book and shade as the sun's heat seems to intensify with every stroke.

As I turn to head back to shore, I grab something in the water. To my horror, I see the head of a jellyfish right beside me.

I scream and everyone around me looks up, watching as I flail in the water. The tide is quite strong now, its grip desperately trying to pull me further and further away from the shore. I shout for my mum, crying, convinced that the jellyfish has followed me, petrified that it will sting me.

'For goodness sake, Madeleine!'

She wades into the water and pulls me back to the shore, her head hanging in embarrassment. The beachgoers are now hysterical, laughing at the sight of a fourteen-year-old girl crying for her mum.

My uncle's laughing too, while my brother shakes his head in embarrassment, keen to get back to throwing the ball around and pretending that we're not related. I hurry back underneath the umbrella, my cheeks pink from embarrassment, but a smile on my face. I watch as my uncle throws around the ball, the biggest smile on his too.

We don't see my uncle that often, usually only for Christmas or holidays as he lives in Spain. But, when we do see him, we all have an amazing time.

'He passed away this morning.'

The glorious beach memory glimmers and then dissipates before my very own eyes.

I'm back. The sun radiates outside, desperately banging against the windows to be let in. The room I'm sitting in now is dark, lifeless. In this moment there is no joy, there is no light.

My stepmum grips my hand tightly as I desperately try to swallow the lump in my throat, squeezing my eyes shut to hold back the river of tears that are about to start flowing. My heart is pounding.

Why him?

It was going to happen; I knew it was. We all knew it was. Skin cancer. In just under a year of being diagnosed, it happened — the unimaginable happened.

I look back to the sunshine outside, the ball of fire menacingly looking back.

I'm hit with emotion: devastation, disbelief, relief that he was no longer in pain; guilt that I hadn't rung him or texted him every single day to catch up and see how he was doing; shock that the last time I had casually waved goodbye to him at the airport was the last time I would see ever see him again.

He's no longer in pain, Mads, I think. *Try to remember that.*

Now, years on, I often find myself thinking of that beach memory. I remember the smile on his face, his laughter, the joy that he radiated.

And you can bet damn well that I'm glad that I went into the water that day.

The yellow envelope

JOY M. MAWBY

I was glad my mum was not a hoarder. Even so, there had been a lot to help her sort out before she moved into the 'Older People's Retirement Apartment' close to where I lived.

It had taken ages to sift through all the photographs and to mount the ones she wanted to keep. There were lots of black and white photos of my father, James (known as Jim) Downs. There were several large ones of him in his RAF uniform, his hat on the side of his head. There were some of him and Mum and some of the three of us. There was one of my cousin Les and me playing hopscotch with Dad. A rather blurred one showed Dad running backwards while I ran forwards. He could easily beat me, whichever way round he ran but somehow he always managed to stumble, just before the finish of the race, so that I was triumphant.

My snap was taken when he was on leave. It showed me sitting on a chair in our little back garden, my head tipped back. Mum's sister, Alice, was standing nearby, smiling. Dad was shampooing my hair from behind. I was laughing at the novelty of it. Dad had worked as a barber and I remembered him saying that the owner of the barbershop was going to have 'backward' basins installed after the war. They were the latest thing.

'I'll make us a cup of tea,' my mother said as I started looking through the very last box, which had resided under her bed. Right at the bottom of it, underneath a pile of letters and cards, was a flat, square box tied with string. On the lid in Mum's handwriting were the words 'Jim's voice'. I untied the string, lifted off the lid and there it lay — a dull black 78 RPM record with its small packet of wooden needles. In a moment, I was back in our old house, in Camberley.

Les and I answer the knock at our front door.

'Who is it?' Mum calls.

'Just a letter,' I shout back.

'Hurry up. The food's on the table.'

It is school dinner time and we are having macaroni cheese. It smells delicious as we run into the kitchen. I hand Mum the yellow envelope, we rinse our hands at the kitchen sink and sit down.

There is a strange silence for a moment. Mum and Auntie Alice are staring at the small sheet of paper Mum has taken out of the yellow envelope. Then she gives a gasp, more a little scream really, and Auntie puts her arm round Mum's shoulders.

'You stay here and eat your dinner,' Auntie says to us. 'We have to go to see Auntie Fran for a few minutes.' Without looking at us, they go out of the back door.

Auntie Fran is not related to us but she lives next door and has known us since we were born so we call her 'Auntie'. She and Mum and are close friends.

'I wonder what the letter was about,' Les says. 'It looks as if it could be serious.

'Mm' I say as we tuck into our macaroni cheese.

Ages later, Auntie Fran comes in without knocking. 'It's time to go back to school now,' she says.

'When are Mum and Auntie Alice coming home?' I ask.

'Don't worry, they'll be here by the time you get back from school. They're busy at the moment.'

We've already washed up our plates but have left, on the table, the other two with helpings of macaroni cheese, grown cold. Auntie Fran covers them with two more plates and something about her face stops us asking any more questions.

That afternoon, Mrs Cartwright, our class teacher, gives out the small papier-mâché dishes we have been making over the past few weeks. Mine is covered in little red, purple and blue flowers which I painted on to the top layer of the newspaper. We varnished the pots in the last art lesson and mine shines prettily. I am proud of it although it is a bit lopsided. I carry it home in triumph at the end of school. I have forgotten all about the letter in the yellow envelope.

I walk the short distance home with my friend Sylvia. Les is in the 'big boys' school' and finishes later. It is very quiet in the kitchen when I go in. Mum is not busy getting the tea or with ironing or with any job at all. She is just sitting. Auntie Alice is not even knitting. I wave my beautiful dish in front of Mum.

'Look, it's finished. Do you like it?' I feel sure this will cheer her up.

'It's beautiful, darling. Well done.'

'It's for Daddy but you can share it.'

There's a pause and then, 'Thank you. That's lovely.'

Her voice sounds different and I wonder if I have upset her. 'You don't mind that it's for Daddy, do you? It's just that he's been away for such a long time.'

'Of course I don't mind, darling.' She gets up suddenly and goes into the front room.

I turn to Auntie Alice. 'I'll put it on the mantelpiece,' I say. 'Mum and you can enjoy looking at it and it will be safe there until Daddy comes home.'

The next day, the postman delivers a flat, square box tied with string.

I just buy a ticket

DIANA LAURA DUCKWORTH

It is the age before we have a telephone or a car.

I am the third child. Unimportant! Tiny! Not pretty. My straight hair is sometimes wet and rolled and twisted up in rags ripped from an outworn sheet, so that, when untied I'll have loose, bouncy tresses. Mousy, silky curls make an attractive difference.

'Put me on the bus,' I tell my mother. 'I want to go to grandma.'

I am three years old.

She doesn't need to hold my hand walking down Abbotsford Hill as we sidle the corners of the zigzag, our route onto the narrow footbridge with wire netting sides. Below the stream is swift. I skip along the pavement and pass the shoe shop display, our doctor's medical room, the grocery shop, and church hall next to the dairy. Here we wait until the afternoon bus lumbers to a stop.

'Hector,' my mother said. 'Put her off at Mum's road end.'

An enormous feeling whooshes through me as my feet climb shiny metal steps, fearlessly, alone. I'm too young to know feelings have names, or why they're instantly there, but this is the moment that changed my life. Something akin to a flame is lit within me. Elation! Sheer magic!

On the single seat near Hector and noisy engine I survey the world before me. The bus begins to move. I sense a peculiar freedom and don't look back. I'm aflame with just 'knowing' — the thrill — I'm leaving, going, and to whom.

An hour or so later the bus slows and stops at a crossroad in country wilderness. There are wire fences, cattle and sky. Hector takes my petite hand in his warm mitt and escorts me across the main tar-sealed highway. My battered suitcase he pokes under the end letterbox of a crooked row of several neighbourly post boxes with red flags, at rest. My case sits atop clumpy soursop weeds.

'Alright?' Hector asks.

I nod, because the case is too heavy for me to lug. He faces me in the right direction then goes to the bus and is gone.

I stare at Maukaatua, the lump of prominence that sleeps like a giant keeping Māori wisdom and secrets. It blots the horizon. The road is a dry snake undulating until disappearing into native bush beautifying its wide bottom. I spy a red roof. It's a lone building cast in the shade of verdant green.

This road, far-seeing, opens before me like a tactile nature book. In the perfect silence I can hear my shoes scrunch gravel. Stones are a roadside hem and the hawthorn hedge a straggly backdrop to unkempt scotch thistles, cocksfoot grass and variegated weeds, russet, tawny and dry. Further on, under tall, twin gum trees, I breathe a different smell. Intoxicating! Fresh! Here I play with gumnuts fallen in the ditch and collect the new-found peaky shaped toys, sticky and cap-like with a texture foreign to me.

Eucalyptus nods to my grandparent's cottage. Across the road I see where Ganga has dumped ash from the fire. I hear music from the talkative creek. Under the ivy archway I half-climb the gate to unlatch the leather fastening. The gate swings open. I *just know* happiness and speed walk beside grandma's garden; a riot of purple asters, mauve phlox, white lilac and violets peeping from heart-shaped leaves growing by the creamery shed. I bring purple to the dark emerald door and knock.

Another moment has arrived — I have arrived.

Curiosity is my forte.

I can navigate the long walk to kindergarten, alone. And I have to pass a white picket fence to pluck purple stock, my favourite colour. Purple makes a bold statement. The kindy teacher is pleased, every time, to receive flower beauty to display on her desk among us local, rowdy chosen children. I love this teacher for her ingenuity.

One hot summer day we children straggle along a clay streak where no houses come into view. We pass forbidden rail tracks and enter an empty paddock. There appears an ugly edifice, a sheep dip filled with odorous, murky water. The teacher gathers us together. Says, 'If one of you children fall in you'll stink forever, and you might drown.' We give it a wide berth — and clutch our billy cans — scatter to find what we've come for. There, along the fence line, growing rampant, prickly and hurtful, are ripe blackberries.

A day or so later, the small glass jar acquired from my mother is returned filled with jam the teacher made from squashed fruit picked by my dainty fingers, stained indigo.

My father called me Crowbar, the family Gypsy Di. My mother never taught fear, but unwittingly gave me the greatest gift of all: the courage key to travel alone, move on, unafraid, and satiate my lust for the unusual. Within me, I carried an inexplicable flame and wore adventure like a second skin. And the *thrill* — of *going* — has never abandoned me.

I've met women and men who questioned. You are not afraid?

I teased. What is there to be afraid of?

How you can travel, alone, to here?

I'd smile.

I just buy a ticket.

My motto: open mind, open heart, open road.

I need to believe

DEBORAH HUFF-HORWOOD

'Nanna, are there really angels?' I ask.

I know she'll say yes; she has so many paintings of them and goes to church every Sunday. I'll ask my real question next.

She laughs softly, radiant in her love for me. 'Of course, darling! Of course there are.'

'What about … fairies?'

'What do you think?'

Her gnarled hand is the most perfectly beautiful hand in my world, clutching mine as we sit on the long, white, wooden bench in her shady courtyard.

'Do you believe in fairies?' she says.

I want to tell her I believe, because I used to, and because Nanna is so much like one, tiny and shimmery and the most perfectly delicate person in the world, her seventy years to my seven.

'I want to believe in them,' I say, 'but I'm not sure. My friend (and I feel hot with cross that she could have said so) said they weren't real.' Somehow a little gulp escapes my throat. I am scared. *Tinkerbell mustn't die!*

Nanna lays her other hand over mine and smooths it, like she smooths the slick, shiny black fur of Rudy the sausage dog. He's asleep under the grandfather clock in the hall. The chimes, every quarter hour, don't stop him snoring. Nanna's fingers are so thin that her ring is almost falling off.

'She just never saw one, darling.'

I turn wet eyes up to her. Wrinkles so deep you can't see their ends crevice her face, thin lips dry with widowhood, not kissed back for so long but kissing us, her grandchildren, left-side-right-side which no one else I know does, just her way of giving more kisses and I love her for it; a meringue of mauve hair caught up on her head like, I imagined, a French ballerina or Russian empress.

She pats my hand, feather taps. 'Shall we? Let's go and have a little look for some.'

With sparkling eyes and a trembling tummy, I skip away and stand at the edge of the garden. I wonder if I should put my sandals on. *No, that might squash the fairies.* Nanna takes a while to rise from the bench but finally stands, swaying a little. I run back and take her hand.

'Which way do we go?' I say.

Nanna makes a beeline for the stone path that leads beneath her Juliet window and down the narrow side of the house, away from the front courtyard that is elegantly designed for entertaining, several doors onto it so the wait staff can come and go, with the big wide front door with its heavy brass knocker nice and low — I can reach it — framed by partitioned glass, everything in symmetrical proportions. Nanna's feet are impossibly narrow, her skin a not-very-nice colour, mottled and spotty from summer after summer after summer; Mummy always makes me wear sunscreen but Nanna's not interested in rubbing it on; 'Too late,' she says with a small smile.

I follow her feet across the sandstone flagstones. Small fleshy plants sprout between these flat islands, and drooping bougainvillea need to be fought off and I'm a bit afraid of getting a spider on my face, especially a dead one; they give me nightmares. The heavy scent of gardenia hits me as I round the corner, no harbour breeze here, the air is caught, hangs timeless, thick and sweet and rich and if I were a fairy I would really like to live here. I bend, my pink dress brushes the dirt and I peer into the sandy-soil spaces beneath the shrubs. Nanna has stopped and watches me with the face of a Madonna.

'That's my bedroom window,' she points, and it is open at the top, fresh air always, 'and Debbie darling, I might have heard them singing one night.'

She looks so delighted; I could burst with adoration for her, for knowing how important this is to me. I desperately need to believe in fairies, Tinkerbell's tiny life depends upon it; I feel mine does too. I have never wanted anything so much.

Nanna says, 'I'm going to look up in these branches.'

She raises frail arms to part the hibiscus and a pale, wizened flower falls and is crunched underfoot as she hunts. She might be singing; I fancy I can hear singing now and am lost in my own little world. The house is built on a steep slope and I take a step up into the next garden bed over small ridges of rock placed there eons ago, rich with tiny brown skinks and generations of sand ants. I carefully step over Nanna's small plants; some struggle to thrive in the grey sand while others cannot be stopped. My fingers prise open the petals of a deep red camellia, then another, and another.

'How small are they?' I call, but don't listen for an answer because there are more flowers, more bushes, more garden beds and I'm travelling up the garden away from her towards the garden gate. And I know, I just know, that fairies live here and if I was a fairy I'd sleep in a flower and I'd choose Nanna's garden and even if I don't find one now it's okay because we're here for weeks and weeks and who wants to watch boring cricket and I'll finish my drawing later, because Nanna has heard fairies in her garden and she believes in them too. She wouldn't let Tinkerbell die and I won't either and one day I am most-very-definitely going to find one.

'Darling?' she calls, and I spin on my bottom, sandy toes grey and fingers caked with dirt, and she is standing down in the courtyard at the side door with her hand on the knob. She has a hungry look about her. 'What about some lunch?'

I gallop down to her. Her eyes sparkle. She stoops, which looks painful for once, to speak in a whisper, so quiet that not even the fairies will be able to hear. 'Did you find anything interesting?'

She hasn't asked directly if I've found any fairies, which is kind, as she knows I haven't or I'd have whooped about it, but I give a little nod and squeeze my lips together, for some secrets are too precious and the doorway is open so my parents might hear. But I reach carefully into the pocket of my dress, then hold out my hand. She looks excited and cradles her fingers beneath mine.

I show her. A tiny silver wing, crisp, pale, dry almost to dust.

With a breathless gasp, her hand flies to her mouth. Tears pool in her eyes, and we reverently, oh-so-delicately, walk together into her bedroom and place the precious wing in a silver case on her dressing table.

Then I wash my hands for lunch.

Two words

DIANE SIMS

The crinkly paper bunched underneath my bottom and the dingy room was dim with one lightbulb. He sat with legs crossed while she perched on the rusting chair.

Turning my eyes to the doctors I spit two words: 'Fuck you.'

And uttering that expletive was the moment that changed my life.

It was a late June evening with young leaves whispering at the window. I was seventeen, a good Baptist girl who loved school, skiing, taught Sunday School and had never dreamt of uttering such vulgarities.

'You have multiple sclerosis, will be in a wheelchair soon, bedridden by 27 and dead by 35,' the specialist in the suit so suavely lipped off.

She, the obsequious resident retorted, 'You have your head screwed on right so we're telling you without your parents present.'

Uttering those two words of rebellion changed me from an adolescent to an adult determined to fight those deafening deadlines.

That night I sat with the nurses in the Toronto hospital wing drinking Earl Grey tea and munching barbecue corn chips. Wisps of ward doctor gossip crept into my web of dread: my parents' reaction, the list of imminent physical losses, friends' reactions.

What shadows, what stumbles were next?

Geez, would I ever have a boyfriend?

The next morning my parents left the doctor's cubicle with grim faces and eyes averted. In their sixties, they were devastated. I had a brother with severe Down syndrome. Now me. Mom, close to my sister who was eight months pregnant, stayed in Toronto with Karen. Dad and I flew home to northern Ontario. His only words on the airplane were a menacing, 'Don't you dare tell your aunts.' In his family sin caused disease, hence his shame.

Friends met me with bouquets of balloons, flowers — and a car. Dad left me and vanished for a week on a bender, so with $5 in my wallet and the hidden house key I learnt to 'get by with a lot of help from my friends'.

To paraphrase Blanche Dubois, 'I am dependent on the kindness of friends'.

My best friend and I arranged for meds to arrive from Arizona, cajoled an ancient doctor into treating me without hospitalization. And with the old red VW Bug full on $3 gas Cindy and I bought burgers and headed to camp. It was 1975. The Vietnam War was ending; mine just beginning.

To fight the disease, I had to get strong. To fight my parents' shame and dismissal of my hopes, I had to be strong. How?

Long before visualization became trendy, I saw the MS as a shadow that at times loomed larger than I was just as at day's end but I trusted it would recede just as morning broke.

Humour helped: 'When God was handing out eggs, I thought he said legs,' so, I quipped, 'I'll take mine scrambled please!'

My parents wanted me to finish high school and stay home, essentially waiting for God. They were at a loss. But the Bible says, 'for when I am weak then I am strong.'

Through more mobility and vision exacerbations I finished two bachelor's degrees, then a master's degree. I worked at a large newspaper the tenth-year anniversary of my diagnosis. That evening fellow reporters rented a van for an all-night pub crawl. First deadline missed amid disco dancing!

A senior newspaper editor told me I'd never advance if the info that I had MS was 'exposed'. Two words.

There remains such discrimination against people physically challenged, an assumption that if the body is impaired so is the mind. I've advocated for employment equality and participated in every eligible MS research project. One paper dubbed me, 'The Indefatigable Ms Sims'.

I worked for sundry national print/broadcast media, finally becoming corporate editor of a government Crown corporation. The age 35 drop-dead deadline passed. Whew! Two words.

Eleven months later my 'annus horribilis' happened, to quote Queen Elizabeth. It was 1996. Years battling MS would stand me in good stead.

In January, my sister Karen, who had been diagnosed with MS a few years previously, died painfully of ovarian cancer. I held my weeping mom in my lap when Karen passed one dreary Sunday.

Our last aunt died and I held Mom's frail hand in church that March afternoon.

A massive stroke killed Mom in May. She unconsciously caressed my thumb before leaving.

The Friday of October Thanksgiving weekend, I landed in emergency surgery at midnight in tremendous angst. I remember thanking the medical team before being anesthetized. A huge tumour was untangled from my abdomen.

'Hey, I just gave birth to a 10-pound turkey this weekend,' I softly teased the next afternoon.

Four days later ovarian cancer was confirmed. I was given a year to live. Two words.

Ensuing months brought six increasingly serious surgeries. I continued to thank medical teams in three different cities.

Other two words joined my battle plans: hold on, hold fast, hold hope, hold hands.

I am no Pollyanna. Complications worsened the MS and increased the pains in my legs. My body is a cancer-scarred roadmap with constant aching. One November night in a hospital room far from home I crept into Mom's intangible arms and begged her to whisk me away.

Yet 'joy' and 'gratitude' became my touchstones.

The next year my first book was published in three countries with a national book tour. When a brother looked at the first copy, he wept — Mom would be so proud. I hoped so.

By that time, I was on the board of directors for the fledgling Canadian ovarian cancer association. I fought nationally alongside women, physicians and scientists against this absolutely insidious cancer that whispers. There is no early detection tool, physicians have little training in this leading, deadly female cancer and women too often dismiss the signs. Education is key.

My next book was the first published on ovarian cancer for women in Canada. An international pharmaceutical company bought copies to send to all ob-gyns across the country.

A Paris pharmaceutical company bought the publishing rights and distributed copies to all ob-gyns in France.

Book royalties have gone to MS and ovarian cancer research and most recently tuberculosis treatment in South Africa.

Since then the cancer has recurred, with many medical and surgical end-dates. I am repeatedly told to prepare. Thoughtfully, two words come to mind.

As a songster sings, I have had the 'chance to live like I was dying', years rich in joy and gratitude.

I never wanted another seventeen-year-old girl, nor another 38-year-old woman told what I was. It is a few decades later and that girl hasn't been given that death sentence thanks to a plethora of MS-arresting drugs. However, it is not yet true for that woman. Soon, I pray.

'Adversity does not build character, it reveals it,' wrote James Lange Allen, as a dear friend often reminds me.

I've walked, fallen down, got up, done it over again. These years I rock and roll in my wheelchair and keep on dancing in my soul!

Remember two words ... and keep fighting.

PART 6
LEARNING MOMENTS

There is no end to education. It is not that you read a
book, pass an examination, and finish with education.
The whole of life, from the moment you are born
to the moment you die, is a process of learning.

Jiddu Krishnamurti

I am always ready to learn although I
do not always like being taught.

Winston Churchill

An intelligent heart acquires knowledge, and
the ear of the wise seeks knowledge.

Proverbs 18:15

History is not what you thought.
It's what you can remember.

1066 and All That, *W.C. Sellar and R.J. Yeatman*

That's what learning is. You suddenly
understand something you've understood
all your life, but in a new way.

Doris Lessing

*M*oments where we learn about ourselves, about others and about the world can present themselves at any time in our lives. Marian Penman's school friend sabotaged her maths test, teaching Marian that 'sometimes you just had to take a deep breath, sit up straighter and carry on'. Looking at an old photograph set the context for Jessica Folk to recall how, as a young child, she 'learnt not to trust'. Jan Davies had her eyes opened by an ex-monk when they met, leaving her with 'a sense of freedom and an overwhelming flood of joy'. Leaving Odessa at nine years old, Orine Ben Shalom started a life of change and learnt about the 'best lie' her parents ever told. Blaine Marchand was told by a perceptive teacher that 'you really could be a writer one day, if that is what you wish'.

All is not fair

MARIAN PENMAN

I was eight.

I had done my homework. I had learnt all the words for the spelling test. So I sat in my usual place, next to Pamela, my best friend. We smiled at each other, confident, pencils poised for the test.

We were clearly destined to be best friends judging by the contrast in our physical appearances. Pamela was blonde, well rounded and extremely pretty. I was rather plain, tall and skinny with straight mousey-brown hair.

We were both Brownies, in the pack run by the teacher administering this spelling test. This teacher lived across the road from us. I had already worked out that she had favourites, and I was not one of them, even though I tried my hardest. All the girls in our class were members of the Brownies; the ones she liked were elves, and all the others, me included, were imps. Pamela was an elf.

I was sad, because I had wanted to be an elf, but my mother had told me it was just random, this girl here, that girl there, and so on. I tried very hard to believe her, because I know my mother wouldn't have had favourites. She was a Sunday School teacher.

In our family we were all favourites; me, because I was the eldest and the only girl, Nigel because he was the first son and the eldest boy, then Adrian, the youngest, always to be special as her last baby, something I fully understood when I became a mother. So although there must have been sibling rivalry, I don't remember it.

My grandparents came to live with us when I was about seven, and Adrian, being the youngest, was Grandad's 'little Robin' and probably the one joy in Grandad's life after Grandma died. Nigel and I were grateful to escape that responsibility.

There was only one television in our house, and that was in Grandad's room. We had to knock on the door and ask if we may watch something. Fortunately, back in the early 1960s there wasn't a choice of programs if you didn't have Independent TV, which you had to pay for. That channel had *Bonanza*, which we would have loved, but even while we tried to watch *The Lone Ranger* on BBC, Grandad would mutter 'Terrible pictures, terrible pictures,' every time a gun was fired.

So Nigel and I mostly played outside games. We had many trees, all of which presented a challenge. The trees with the low branches became our circus. We were acrobats, swinging from branch to branch. A higher tree with a U-shaped branch was a camel on which we rode, like Lawrence of Arabia, into the desert. We had pirate ships, we had our 'dens'.

One day, in my competitive determination to be better, I climbed to the very highest branches of the horse chestnut tree, only to look down and panic. My lovely dad had to get a ladder and rescue me, for I was frozen to the branch.

But in our outdoor games, we apparently made a lot of noise, disturbing the peace of the neighbourhood. We made go-karts from whatever pieces of wood we could find around. Nigel even took the wheels off my doll's pram but I acquiesced if I could have the first ride.

Our house was situated at the top of a steep hill, so biking and go-karting were an obvious activity. Pamela wasn't keen on those things, so when I went to her house we played with our dolls. It was so much more fun playing dolls with a friend. My brothers were useless. Just not interested. Was that due to the gender indoctrination of the time? Didn't matter. I had balance.

Thus, most of the time I joined in the games with my brothers and their friends. Our go-karts crashed so we made another, on which we screamed our way down the hill. We understood that the last, steepest part of the drive went straight into a main road, so we had to rein in and pull to the left as we approached the danger point. Which we did. We didn't want to die.

But clearly, our juvenile games were too noisy for some people because my mother was very upset to receive an anonymous complaint from a neighbour, saying that her children were too noisy. We tried to keep quiet, we really did. It transpired that the complainant was none other than my school teacher.

School was important to me. I did my homework, over and above; total nerd. I relished spelling tests. Not so much mental arithmetic, but that's another story.

So there I was, pencil poised, smiling at my bestie, when the test started.

All done, I confidently passed my paper to Pamela for marking, as she passed hers to me. We went through it all, marked it and handed it back.

I was devastated.

There was an error. That could not be possible. I looked through it and was horrified. An 'o' had been changed to an 'a'.

My hand shot up. My teacher barely raised her eyes.

'This is wrong,' I said, confused.

'Don't try to cheat,' said my teacher.

I looked at Pamela. She met my gaze, gave a smirk and put her 20 out of 20 paper in her desk.

That was the moment that changed my whole approach to life, the moment when I realized that life was not fair; that it was no good throwing a tantrum, having a hissy fit. It was pointless fighting for explanations and closure. Sometimes you just had to take a deep breath, sit up straighter and carry on.

The 4x6 photograph

JESSICA L. FOLK

I wish I could talk to her.

That sweet little girl in the photo, not quite four years old, ringlet curls spilling over the shoulders of her pale pink Lambchop sweatshirt. That girl who smiled down at the brand-new baby with all the love an older sister is born to carry.

I wish I could talk to her.

I wish I could warn her — that young, happy child, her rosy-cheeked brother, her sister so new to the world — and her mother, sweetly leaning down with the fresh, still swollen infant, her light pink bathrobe such a soft and cheery colour against the grey of the hospital walls.

I wish I could warn them all.

It's remarkable the capacity photographs have to freeze time. They're a snippet of a memory — one frame, one moment in time. They capture every visible thing in front of them.

But what do they miss? What don't they see? What exists beyond that 4x6 print? What did they all forget to see as the camera focused on them, on this seemingly happy family in the maternity ward of the hospital that cold day in 1994?

What they didn't see was the father in the hallway, just the day before, saying hello to his mistress. A hello that would forever be captured on the home video they'd uncover years later in a dusty pile of VHSs marked 'memories'. It was another staring camera, another lens, another truth revealed.

There's irony there.

That the man who filmed that video of his mistress and other co-workers would, hours later, capture the aftermath of the birth of his third child, his last with my mother, and proclaim that he was happy.

Maybe this was how the little girl learnt to lie.

What she doesn't know is that her family will irreparably break a few months after this picture is taken. That she, her brother and her little sister will eventually visit the woman from the home video in her apartment where the little girl's father moved into after her parents split. That she'd spend mornings sitting on the floor of that unfamiliar home eating Reese's puffs and other too-sugary cereals with a man who used to sleep in the same bed as her mother. What she doesn't know is that this new woman in her father's life will be a mere pit stop in a string of relationships that carries on for more than a decade.

This was how the little girl learnt not to trust.

She doesn't yet worry that she's a walking cliché of a girl from a broken home. She doesn't yet eat everything in sight, hoping to stuff down the sadness and the guilt of feeling like she failed in some way. She doesn't yet date someone who resembles her father in all the wrong ways, perhaps subconsciously hoping to get some piece of her past back. She doesn't see the irony. She doesn't hurt.

She doesn't feel her stomach drop at the idea that the only things she'll ever write worth reading will be about her father. He's always there in every story she writes, even the made-up ones. Maybe that's because he always seemed to be there, even when he wasn't. Maybe it's how he enters so many dinner conversations when he hasn't talked to any of them for months. Maybe it's because he taught her to love stories — planting her in front of countless films and books while he slept on the couch after a long day on call at the same hospital where he broke her family.

She'll have to work really hard not to hate herself for loving the things he loves.

In a way, this little girl is free. Free to think that this new baby is a perfect representation of goodness in the world. Free to think that life will always be joyful. Free to imagine that change is not a threat and that her family will always look like this.

There is a lot of pain in growing up and seeing your own childhood from a new perspective. I don't remember being unhappy — not as a young kid. I barely remember the bitter sting of the pain of losing this version of my family. I don't know when I stopped being the carefree young girl in that photo. I have this evidence of a family that was not yet broken — a 4x6 photograph of a new beginning. I have proof of a family on the precipice of something new.

This photograph is evidence of the family we'd become. No father in sight. A mother who would always be right there, supporting us through every decision, every failure and every joy.

Along the way, I may have learnt not to trust, to lie, and how to move through pain. But I also learnt how to love, how to care for others, how to live a life I can be proud of and reach for what I want. I didn't learn those things from him. I learnt them from her. And from that little girl — filled with so much happiness and possibility, looking down at her little sister with the kind of love that is captured in a fleeting moment, in a photograph, a love that just might carry her through everything.

A pilgrimage

JAN DAVIES

On the evening of my arrival in Porto I walked up the steep hill from the square and noticed a man peering into the window of a second-hand bookshop. He produced a long lens camera and began snapping away. I slowed my step to stare. In a moment the stranger was at my side explaining how he loved old bookshops. He invited me to look through the window. Sure enough, there were thousands of books of various sizes and colours stacked, apparently haphazardly, in precarious piles inside the store. I had to agree it was an interesting subject for a photograph.

He introduced himself as Willy from Switzerland. His first language was German but he spoke perfect English. Standing at least 6 feet 3 inches tall, with high forehead, fair hair and amiable features, he was a striking gentleman. We discovered we were booked on the same Douro river cruise the day after next. Will smiled, shook my hand warmly and wished me a good night.

A walking tour around the city took up most of the following day. A local guide ushered a group of us from church to monument, culminating at Porto Cathedral. Here, the Way of Saint James pilgrims begin their journey to the Cathedral of San Diego de Compostela in Galicia, north-west Spain, where the Tomb of the Apostle St James is believed to lie. Camino de Santiago, or Saint James' Way, crosses Portugal from south to north and is known as the Northern Way. 'The cult of this saint,' said our guide, 'became popular during the Middle Ages, resulting in great pilgrimages from every corner of Europe.' We walked down the first few hundred steep, well-trodden stone steps where local women were hanging out their washing.

On the day of the river cruise, Will nodded a greeting as we queued to embark under the hot sun. Once on deck I made my way to a shady spot and prepared to enjoy the excursion. My brochure explained that the 210-kilometre river had been treacherous to navigate before the nineteenth century until dams were built between Porto and Barca d'Ava. Hand-built terraces of port wine vineyards sloped along the water's edge. Shades of emerald and sky blues reflected in the still water. Further upriver we would be negotiating the famous locks of Crestuma and Carrapatelo.

After a while Will joined me. It transpired he had just completed the Saint James' Way pilgrimage — a lifelong ambition of his. He told me his parents, devout Roman Catholics, had sent him to a monastery in

Switzerland from a very young age as he had shown academic prowess and a deep interest in all things religious and spiritual. He spent eight years as a novice monk, preparing for a devotional life within the cloisters. But now he had a wife and four grown-up children and was flying to Geneva that very evening to be reunited with his family after six months.

I wanted to ask him about his decision to leave the monastery. But such questions to a virtual stranger would seem impertinent. I closed my eyes and pondered the question of celibacy imposed on men in religious orders.

'I heard about the Camino Santiago pilgrimage as a boy,' continued Will. 'Even before Christian times the route existed for pilgrims. Stargazers saw in the Milky Way what they thought was a map of the end of the world. So the pilgrim's journey continues to the Atlantic coast of Galicia, ending in Cape Ministered [literally Land's End, in Latin].'

There was a certain magnetism about this man. His voice was hypnotic. He had the personality and charisma I once expected of Jesus although he looked nothing like the Jesus of my childhood storybooks. While admiring his courage and determination to 'be a pilgrim' I couldn't help wondering how his family could bear to let him out of their lives for so long. Bizarrely, the song *I Don't Know How to Love Him*, supported by full orchestra, began playing in my mind.

Will continued to explain that any pilgrimage, in its true sense, is a journey to a holy place to obtain supernatural help through penance or thanksgiving.

'Ideally, pilgrims adhere to the Codex Calixtinus,' he said. 'The pilgrim's route is the lack of vices, the thwarting of the body, increase in virtues, pardon for sins, sorrow … protection from the heavens. The pilgrimage takes us away from luscious food … gluttonous fat vanishes, restrains voluptuousness, constrains appetites of the flesh … humbles the haughty … rewards those who live simply and do good works.'

He then took a beautiful scallop shell from his haversack and placed it in my palm.

'This is the symbol of Camino de Santiago. Legend has it that the body of Saint James was lost during a heavy storm but was washed ashore intact, protected by a covering of scallops.'

I traced the rim of the shell with my fingers. 'They meet at a single point,' he demonstrated, sliding his index finger along each pink mother-of pearl groove. 'These marks are symbolic of the various routes pilgrims travel to meet at one destination.'

Will cupped the scallop shell between my hands and smiled. 'Keep it. Just as waves of the ocean wash scallop shells on to the shores of Galicia, so the hand of God guides pilgrims to Santiago.'

As we went through the Crestuma Lock I wondered why Will had in fact been 'guided' by God to abandon monastic orders. Perhaps he had discovered 'the loving relationship between men and women' as Leonard Cohen had during his time as a Buddhist monk. But as we began our descent into the Carrapatelo Lock, daylight suddenly faded to darkness, the air became still and humid and the only sound was of rushing water. My mood plummeted and a cold terror gripped me. We were descending into death's watery pit. I was trapped, heading for the Realm of Hades, plunging into the watery Micatin underworld of the Aztecs; falling headlong into Hell. Everything was disappearing into the stifling blackness. We were hemmed in on both sides by towering walls. Struggling to breath, I closed my eyes against a spinning world and was plunged into a dark chasm.

It was over in a few moments but as we returned from the darkness into the sunlight I could actually see myself sitting on the deck, far below. I was conscious of being returned to my body and restored by gravity to my original posture. With feet firmly on deck and my back against my chair, I looked around for Will. He was engrossed in a conversation but turned to smile reassuringly at me. His face was calm, beautiful and serene. Here was a man at peace with life. A sense of freedom and an overwhelming flood of joy enveloped me. Whatever had sustained Will so far on life's journey would sustain me throughout mine. The scallop shell in my hand reminds me that I once crossed paths with 'a god amongst men'.

Leaving

~

ORINE BEN SHALOM

The immigration began years ago. It was 1990; I was nine, and the city was hot and humid. Odessa, the pearl of the Black Sea, was always humid, even during the chilly September evenings of the 1990s, before the USSR collapsed and blood flooded the streets. Momma picked me up from school and suggested we hop all the way home. It was always her way to apologize to me after a screaming session, or doing something fun together when she felt sad. We passed the statue of my beloved Atlases holding the sky on their backs and I waved to them.

At home Papa waited in the 'room' that was both their bedroom and our living room and dining room. On the table was a jug of tea and Baba

Fanya's oatmeal cookies. Momma sat down on my side of the table and asked Papa to start talking. He started from afar, from the history of mankind, through quotes from books we loved together, and then told me that we, the whole family, were Jews. I had no idea. So Momma got into the conversation and said that as Jews, we had the opportunity to fly on a plane to Israel and go on interesting adventures on another continent. I wanted to go pee and think about it. Just before I got up, Papa said he wanted to stay in Odessa, for a short time, because there were things he could only do here.

It was the best lie they ever told us, me and my brother 'Piglet'. That Papa will only stay a little longer in Odessa and join us very soon. Their divorce happened above our heads, when the humid autumn turned into wet winter, with no ginger leaves on the pavement to soften our hops. Nor did we hop any more, as sadness took away the pep of my Momma's step.

For one year in my life I was a 'stinky Jew'.

By the spring of 1991 it was already Ukraine and I would never again have a homeland, just a hometown that was still hot and humid and no longer welcoming. A second before we left, Grandma asked us to sit for a moment. An old Russian superstition. You must sit for a moment before a journey, for lucky travels and a safe return. I got up excitely and ran outside. Momma and Grandma took out the last bags and the big men loaded them quietly on the bus. I never saw a bus in the middle of the night, let alone on Grandma's little street. Momma asked that both me and Piglet go to the bathroom before setting out, because the road was going to be long. I grabbed Piglet's warm hand and we ran upstairs to pee. When we returned, more families were standing around the bus, and the big men were working in complete silence loading the bags. There were far more bags, suitcases, sacks and boxes than there were people. There was very little light, and I was sure this was a sign of a great adventure, not of a quiet disappearance of my childhood. Except for me and Piglet, I only saw one more child. He cried and insisted not to get on the bus.

Piglet and I got on quickly to grab the best spot, the first row on the right, just behind the driver. It is possible in this row to push with your feet and it does not hurt anyone, because the driver is behind a small wall. I was sitting by the window because I wanted to see and remember everything, especially the plane! After we sat down, me by the window and Piglet next to me, they loaded more bags and boxes next to us. It was already a little less comfortable and fun, but at least the whining kid was sitting far away from us.

I have not sat by the window since. Piglet fell asleep, and I missed the few pee stations that the stone-faced guards reluctantly offered us. Twenty-four hours' restraint. Papa drove in a car with a friend to the border with Moldova. The last time I hugged him I told him he had a year to come, and after that I would have no dad. He swore he would come.

After that there was another drive to Bucharest and a hotel. Green ice-cream that I did not get to taste but only to watch the whining kid eat with a grin, spilling it from the corner of his mouth. The long journeys in elevators with mirrors. Huge beds and hot tap water. First time in my life the water remained hot.

As we approached our final destination, I was peeling off layer after layer of all the clothes they had me wear through customs, and Momma kept hissing that nice girls didn't walk around in tank tops. Then the entrance to the huge hall at the airport and the bag of sweets I had never seen before.

The following years I was a 'stinky Russian'.

I saw Papa again at the age of 22. I told him I forgave him. He died six months later.

The weave of words and images

BLAINE MARCHAND

I looked up from my notebook splayed out in front of me, scanned the clock to see what remaining time was left. Below it, Mrs Davis was perfectly framed by the square of blackboard behind her. Across the dark slate, in her elegant cursive handwriting, which I struggled to copy but mine was always a sprawled series of jerks and slants, was the topic she had assigned to us: from their prison cell, one man looked up and saw stars; the other looked down and saw mud.

I was light-headed from the consternation of putting thoughts to paper. It was as if I were coming to the surface of water after holding my breath as I plunged deeper down into its murky depths. I turned my head towards the window where, beyond the pane of glass, December's late afternoon sky was already beginning to be immersed in darkness.

Just two months earlier, in mid-October, Mrs Davis stood before us in a tweed suit, each hand holding the other, her arms crafting a V in front of her jacket and skirt. She cleared her throat and in a pleasant voice began:

Along the line of smoky hills
The crimson forest stands,
And all the day the blue-jay calls
Throughout the autumn lands.

The lines sent a thrill, a current, through my eleven-year-old body. They were so vivid, so descriptive and exactly like the solitary walks I took at this time of the year in the bush by the river at the end of our street.

It was a wild sort of place, crosshatched in light and shadow, sudden echoes of bird call, their clicks, chucks, whirrs and whines, from within the deep red canopy towering over me. The woods were a comforting, private space. They took me away from the hurly-burly of our small house, bursting at the seams with two parents and eight boisterous children.

I repeated the opening lines to myself and wondered — how did the writer decide on these images? He was like a painter sketching out a scene. After a pause, Mrs Davis continued:

Now by the brook the maple leans

With all his glory spread,

And all the sumachs on the hills

Have turned their green to red.

The words and their rhythm, which Mrs Davis' recital released into the air, were like migrating birds fleeing the sudden arrival of cold temperatures. Her lips shaped sounds, so pitch perfect, that they emphasized and enriched the poem as her voice flowed from line to line, building like the swell of a wave.

Is this something I could do? I asked myself. Four years ago, I had hidden one of my school notebooks under my mattress of the lower bunk bed. In the evening, while my brothers and sisters watched TV, that new-fangled device our father had bought and set up near the front window — better here for reception, he said, as he jangled the rabbit ears back and forth — I would slip up to the bedroom the five boys shared and take out my notebook and fill it with the scribbles of a new story, always of animals possessing human characteristics, trying to resolve some dilemma in their lives.

Listening to Mrs Davis, I saw this poem possessed magic, a spark that my stories did not have. Why didn't they? They fell flat as the stones I dropped into puddles. How could I learn about poetry, its weave of words and images that lifted it off the page and into an imaginary place?

Mrs Davis' shoulders rose up and with gusto her hands parted, lifted like wings:

Now by great marshes wrapt in mist,
Or past some river's mouth,
Throughout the long, still autumn day
Wild birds are flying south.

A moment of silence and then Mrs Davis announced to us that she loved poetry and would recite one each day until Christmas break, explaining to us afterwards how and why it spoke to her. My heart skipped like a pebble repeating across a bay.

I put my pencil down, leaned my head into my fingertips. I had no more to say about stars and mud. I had no experience of prison. But I was determined. Before beginning, I took a deep breath and let myself be absorbed into the cold, dank stones that confined the narrow room, the bars securing the tiny opening onto the outside world, and the tension in the hands of each man as they held onto the shafts, looked out into the yard and called up their past and wondered about their future.

I decided to read over what I had written, searching for spelling mistakes or errors in grammar that Mrs Davis always circled with her ruby pen. Was there sparkle in this essay? Had I caught the mood and thoughts of the two men as they looked out through the rods in their window? I chided myself it simply was not good enough.

A hand was suddenly on my left shoulder, the fingers gently squeezing it. I raised my head and there was Mrs Davis at the left-hand side of my desk. How long had she been standing in the aisle? I covered my notebook in shame at my handwriting, my attempt at a story. She moved my hand away and kept reading. Terror seized me. I began to shake.

She moved a little ahead to face me square on. She smiled at me. 'You know, you really could be a writer one day, if that is what you wish.'